ZACH TOUCHON

You Have Everything You Need To Get What You Want

HOW TO UNCOVER THE RESOURCES
RIGHT IN FRONT OF YOU.

YOU HAVE THE POWER TO
CHANGE EVERYTHING!

©zachtouchon

Published by Touchon Publishing Los Angeles

Print ISBN: 978-1-66783-824-3
eBook ISBN: 978-1-66783-825-0

Cover design by Zach Touchon.

Author is independent of all agencies.

@zachtouchon
zachtouchon@gmail.com

**I want to thank my wife,
Ekaterina Khrustaleva Touchon,
without whom none of this
would have been possible.**

I would also like to thank all of my friends and family
for supporting me on my journey
to realize my dreams.

Dedicated in loving memory to my momma,

Elizabeth Touchon.

Why Did I Write This Book?

Like me, you may be searching for a breakthrough to help you take your life to the next level. When I began writing this book, I was looking for a new perspective, a new truth that would set me free. Are you trying to find that one piece of the puzzle that will pull it all together and create the beautiful life that you want? You may be in the right place.

This isn't a book about some multimillion-dollar pyramid dream. I'm not going to promise you a fancy car or a big house or that you can get rich quickly by reading this book. What I am offering is a set of tools and principles that will help you discover what you want and how you can get it. Using these tools and principles, you will be able to identify your strengths and weaknesses and discover one simple truth:

YOU ALREADY HAVE EVERYTHING YOU NEED TO GET WHAT YOU WANT!

How did I discover this truth for myself?

I have acted in almost forty movies, run my own art gallery, sold thousands of dollars' worth of art, written several feature screenplays, become an executive producer, recorded hundreds of songs, and started and run a successful company on the Westside of Los Angeles. I have a beautiful wife, I live on the beach in California, and I'm happy, fulfilled, financially independent, self-made, and I do what I love doing every day. Most importantly, I am proud of who I am.

It wasn't always that way. I grew up in a bad neighborhood, what many would call "on the wrong side of the tracks." I mowed lawns, waited tables, was a cook, worked at all types of manual labor jobs, moved pianos, lived under a bridge and at a shelter for kids when I was homeless at sixteen, lived in a closet, in my car, and endured all types of struggles that made me who I am today. Through those experiences, I never stopped dreaming and wanting a better life. Everything that happened then had to happen for me to be where I am today.

My brother-in-law Chuck has been a mentor and inspiration to me as I have become a man over the last fifteen years. I have a tremendous amount of respect for him.

Naturally, when I decided to write this book, I told him about it. He asked me, "Why are you doing this? What's the plan?"

I paused for a moment and then said, "I am writing this book to find out more about myself, tell my story, and dive into what I can do to get to the success that I want and understand what I need to do to get there. Then, I can use this information to help others get there as well."

The reason I wrote this is so that I could realize that I had everything I needed to get what I wanted. I have read many self-improvement books and always loved how they made me feel. When

I would pick up a good book and find answers that I needed at that moment, it would push me to keep going. I love that. I was looking for the motivation to reach greater heights and successes than I ever thought I could accomplish.

I wanted to create a guide that would contain some practical tools and practices that I could use in my own life to help me reach the fulfillment, success, and happiness I've always dreamed of. Ultimately, I wrote this book to map out a new part of myself and my life. I want to pay closer attention to the details that helped me survive as a creative entrepreneur, but, more importantly, some of the things that have held me back. In the beginning, I was writing this for myself. What I quickly discovered was that others, like you, the one reading this book right now, could benefit from this knowledge as well.

I believe that just a small shift of perspective can be the key to unlocking the potential around and inside of you. I hope that by the end of this book, you will have an entire paradigm shift and gain a set of tools to help you uncover the resources right in front of you. We have everything we need to get what we want, so all we have to do is see it. Join me on this journey to discover the truth that,

YOU HAVE THE POWER TO CHANGE EVERYTHING!

The Journey Begins

We all have a story to tell. There are struggles, failures, successes, pain, losses, good and bad decisions we have made, and so many things that we go through in our lives that make us the people we become. No matter where you are in the world reading this book, I want you to know that your story is important too and that you are the writer of your story. As the writer, you can change the next chapter in your life, just like I did.

This is where my journey begins...

In 2016, I was living the dream. The apartment I was living in was stunning. It had a million-dollar view overlooking the Staples center in Downtown Los Angeles. I was making a lot of wealthy friends. I was living the good life, but none of it was mine. My godfather was letting me crash at his place. I was painting in a studio that my friend let me use, and I was skating by, but I wanted so much more. It looked great from the outside, and it was a great time with no regrets. As I stood there looking out of the floor-to-ceiling window, it felt like I was on top of the world. But I knew that if I wanted to take life on and start having something that was mine, I was going to have to make some dramatic changes.

I had just begun a new romantic relationship with a "big-time Hollywood producer," and we were heading to New Zealand to make a movie. I could see all of the pieces falling into place. I've always been led by my dreams and been willing to drop everything and run towards them. Even if you can't drop everything and run towards your dreams, you still have to be willing to take the next step in your life as well, even if it isn't going to be easy. You have to be willing to step out of your comfort zone and step into your new life or you are forever going to be bound by who you have always been.

We landed at the airport and, within a couple of days, I could already see that it was going to be a bumpy ride. I was in a relationship with the producer, so it was a strange place to be where I had to balance my opinion and what to do between the producer and the director. Other than the fact that I had done several films at that point from the limited view of "talent," this was the first time I was able to see the whole picture from the production side as well. I did what I could do knowing what I knew at that point. Long story short, the film didn't work out. But what I did get is a crash course in filmmaking that, although I didn't know it at the time, would change my life forever. In retrospect, knowing everything I know now, after all I have learned since then, there was way more I could have done. We all do this as we get older; we look back over our experiences and think how we could have done better knowing what we know now. Let's face it, that is not the way life is. There is nothing we can do about the past except learn from it and do our best to do better in the future. Sometimes the most valuable thing that we gain from an experience is the lessons that we learn.

After the disappointment of what could have been a great experience, we flew to Fiji for a quick hiatus before heading back to Los

Angeles. When we got there, it was raining so much that we could barely see the road in front of us. The airport had lost our luggage and we were having a very bad argument. By the time we got to our hotel, we were both ready to break up and move on with our lives. She went off to bed and I went out to let off some steam and make the best of it.

The next morning, I got the news. My mother died. I broke down in disbelief as I ran straight towards the beach. My heart was racing because I was so angry. I was in denial; I could not believe it, and the pain was unimaginable. I fell down to my knees as the waves rushed over me and I began to sob. I would never be the same. Everything had changed.

It's hard to explain the feelings you have at a moment like this even when looking back on it. At the time, your mind is racing and your feelings are all over the place. When you have a loss like this, it's not something you ever really recover from. It gets better over time, but the loss is always there with you. You even come to a place where you like crying and missing them. I had lost many of my friends at this point and that pain was bad, but nothing compared to the loss of my mom. My mother was a guiding light for me and the person I would call when I needed the unconditional love that she always gave me. We would talk nearly every day, sometimes just to say hello. All of a sudden, I was all alone. At least that is how it felt. Where do I go from here? Who do I ask for advice? Who can I make proud? Where will I call home? Who will be there when I'm at my worst? Whose shoulder will there be to cry on?

My girlfriend at the time had us on the next plane to Texas to see my Mom one last time before her body was given over to science.

We made it with just five minutes to spare. In my memory, all of this happens in slow motion. Walking down the long, cold, fluorescent-lit hall towards the room to view the body, knowing this was the last time I would see my Momma. Seeing her laying there on the cold metal bed was surreal. I felt like she would wake up when I touched her cold hand. I just said, "Mom, wake up." The crying was uncontrollable. Even now, writing this, tears are rolling down my face. My brother, my two sisters, and I were there together. My brother began to cry and cry, something none of us had ever seen before. I had moments in the past where I wondered if he even loved her because of his ability to not show emotions, but in that moment, I realized that he loved her and missed her just as badly as the rest of us. That was the beginning of the healing that would happen because of her loss. I was devastated. Losing her was not only a blow to my life, but it also left me in a state of being completely numb. I was lost. The feeling of powerlessness was unbearable.

Somehow, we all found the strength to carry on. Life must go on after all. At the funeral, we discovered what an impact my mother had made on so many people's lives. One after another wanting to tell their stories. Friends of mine who she had helped in their recovery. Friends of hers who she had been there for at their rock bottoms. People she had helped as a nurse. So many people wanted to say thank you that we had to eventually tell them that we were out of time. We all knew mom was a special, giving person, but we had no idea that through the years, day in and day out, she was helping others overcome what she had been through. When I say many, I mean in the hundreds; she was truly a force for helping others and it blew us all away. I sang a song I had written for her and somehow made it through without crying. Then, like a door closing, it was over.

My two sisters and I packed up our childhood home that mom had sold just before she died. It was really difficult to make it through it but we did it and we did it together. My sisters Brittany, Kimber, and I would take turns on memory row crying and crying. Then we had the U-Haul packed and the house was empty and that was that. My childhood was over.

My mom left me a small amount of money, which felt like a lot more than it was. I had quit my side gig to do the movie. In other words, I was unemployed. Then my mom died. There I was with this new girlfriend, and we had an idea, we should open a studio and gallery in Downtown Los Angeles. You see, just about a week before my mom died, she told me, "Zach, I want you to stay with your girlfriend for a while and let her guide you. It won't make much sense and it won't be easy. You have to trust me on this. It will all make sense in time." Little did I know at that moment, but this would be one of the last things she told me. Today, it all makes sense.

The idea was to create a space where we would create full time. We would have a gallery to show the art, and the rest of the place could be a film studio. With all of her connections and my skills, we should have been able to pull together something that could have worked great. My job was to build the space. Her job was to bring in the business.

We found a space at a fantastic price for Los Angeles and, I thought at the time, we had plenty of money. I realized that I was unqual-ified to open a studio. I was an artist. I was painting houses on the side. Although it was going pretty well, at that exact moment, I had nothing going. There I was with some money and I had nothing but time on my hands. I was going through a hard time dealing with the loss of my mom. When I stopped to think, I was worried I would make the wrong decision and end up dead broke with nothing but blurred memories. I couldn't let my mom down.

I could get a job, travel, I could create, I could sit around and do nothing and get drunk all day, or I could give it everything I had to make my dreams materialize. I was going to run out of money any way I looked at it. I didn't want the guilt of losing all of my inheritance living it up. I also didn't want to miss out on making a move while I could. I knew this was a shot to test myself and see how far I could take it. So, after a lot of prayers and asking people if I should do it, we pulled the trigger. That was the beginning of one of the most challenging times in my life so far.

The whole space was a complete disaster. At the time, I didn't realize how bad it was. I was very optimistic about a short completion time. As it turns out, it was way worse than I thought it was when we committed. I was all alone in the construction and, as it turned out, I didn't have as much experience as I believed I did looking back.

There has never been a great warrior who has never faced a battle. Being in the trenches of the battlefield of life gives us the experience to become the great warrior in our lives. Is it messy at times? Do some feelings get hurt? Yes, but we emerge stronger than we were before. I didn't know it at the time, but this experience in the early days of the gallery, when it was all falling apart, would ultimately set me up with the skills to increase my earning power to levels beyond everything I had ever earned before.

Imagine a place that has been vacant for years, located in a newly gentrifying area of Downtown Los Angeles. Since the 1970s, downtown had declined so badly that it was the last place your average well-to-do person would want to live. The exterior of the building was vandalized and covered in graffiti and the windows were all boarded up. As I began tearing the place to pieces, I was quickly going to discover that I was in over my head. The three-month projection turned into four and then five and then finally close to complete in six months. But the truth is, the work would never end. It was just the beginning of a long three years of intense work.

Looking back on this experience, I can see that I was using work as a sort of therapy. I think a lot of people do this but just don't realize it. I couldn't face my grief, so I just worked, and worked, and worked. I was torturing myself in a way, not that it makes any sense. I created my own little prison to cage myself in and sometimes would lose days and days of time locked away inside my gallery working alone.

I understand now that it may be unhealthy to do it the way that I did it, but I think the lesson I learned is that instead of sitting around mourning, I dove in to create something, and when the sadness was finally coming to an end, I looked back and I had an accomplishment. I used mourning as a way to make myself push harder than I had ever pushed before.

A lot of the time, people tend to get crippled by this kind of deep sadness and do nothing. We want to lock ourselves in our room and just be sad and that's OK, but it's not OK forever. When it is all over, we have nothing to show for that time. So, if you are going through deep loss, find ways to use that to create something. It doesn't have to be a great achievement or a big business or anything like that.

Maybe it's a journal, art work, a book, or something you have when it has finally passed. Find a project and use that as therapy. Also, if you feel like you need help, then reach out and get some therapy as well. Use every tool you can to help you grow from loss.

To make matters worse, my partner and I started having serious relationship problems only a couple of weeks into construction. We were arguing over stupid stuff and we were having a hard time getting on the same page. All of her connections dissolved, people didn't show, films lost financing, and on and on. The film business is tough in Los Angeles and it can chew you up and spit you out. People are big talkers, but it takes a lot of filtering through BS to get anywhere. I know this isn't new information, but it's the truth, and if you have been through it, you will know exactly what I am talking about. We realized that, when you put your money where your mouth is, you find out a lot about people, and often when the going gets going, you find yourself all alone. To be honest, I think this may be true for most businesses.

Now, we were six months in, worn out, and going broke fast. On top of it all, we were having a miserable time. My partner, as it turns out, was never going to be on the same page with me. At the time, this made me hate her. Looking back, I am grateful for the lessons one can only learn in the school of hard knocks.

There I was with it all on the line; I was running out of money and my stress was through the roof. My partner wasn't bringing in any business, I had nothing going on, and no idea where to start. Remember, my job was to build the place, but I soon discovered that if you are the boss, your job is everything and I mean everything.

No matter what happens, it is always your fault. No matter how you look at it, it's your problem.

I had to do something, and I had to do something fast because if I didn't, I was going to not only lose everything, I was also going to go into debt and maybe even go bankrupt, and I had just started out. What a nightmare! I was lost in the mess. I felt horrible, and I just wanted to give up. But giving up was never an option.

I was blaming everybody. My partner, my friends, my dad, my godfather. I even started to blame God and my creativity for getting me into this mess. I remember thinking, "if I wasn't an artist, this wouldn't be happening to me." I was sitting in my recording studio looking at all the stuff I had acquired. That's when it hit me. I needed an attitude adjustment.

I had it all, everything I needed, I just had to see it.

CHAPTER 1

What Do You Want?

At first, this question seems like it has a simple answer, right? What do you want? It can be a simple question with a simple response. Or, it can be a tough question you struggle to answer for years, if not a lifetime. Finding what it is that you want in a world full of choices can be difficult. On the other side of the coin, it can be crystal clear in your mind. It can be the center of all your thoughts. It can be your strongest desire. It can be the thing that keeps you up at night and gets you up early in the morning.

When talking to a friend about this, I said,

"I'm feeling lost. I feel like I have no idea what I want."

He responded, "Yes you do. You tell me all the time. What do you want? Say it out loud."

After a long pause, I said, "I want to be a rockstar. I want to be internationally famous. I want a hit record and I want to sell all of my art. I want my gallery to be successful. What I want is to 'make it' doing what I love, being creative. I want to feel free without any financial pressure. I want to create and not feel guilty about it."

What did my buddy say? He said, "That's right. Now, what are you gonna do about it?"

When I said that I wanted to be all of those things, those were the first to come to mind. **When you are thinking about what you want, think as big as you want to.** There are no restrictions or guidelines for this initial part. Imagine that you can do anything and be anyone you want to be. Let your mind just be free and visualize what you want. You don't have to be realistic or consider only those things that you believe are possible. That is one of the limitations we place on ourselves. We only let ourselves think in the realm of possibility that we currently understand. Imagine for a moment that, at this point, you don't have any idea what is possible or impossible. Let the child inside of you just dream. This is where it all starts.

So, *take out a pen and paper and write down what you want*, taking into consideration what I just said. Do you want to be a rockstar? A millionaire? A scientist? An entrepreneur? Do you want to fall in love or reignite the relationship that you already have? Maybe you just want to be happy and fulfilled. *Whatever you want right now. Write it down.*

Now, let's rewind to the first time I got to Los Angeles...

In 2010, I was living in a closet in Playa del Rey. It was a huge step up from the car I was sleeping in previously. I had been in LA for about six months and was a waiter at a corporate Italian restaurant. I was having a great time figuring out how to survive in Los Angeles. I was young and looking for the purpose of my life. I was making it work, and it was a hell of a time. I came to Los Angeles to pursue my hip hop career, but my dad got me a guitar that year, and I was living with actors, so my dream was slowly changing and expanding.

My sister had joined the Peace Corps and was going to be stationed in a small country in Africa. I moved off to California to "blow up," at least that's what I called it at the time. It had been about a year and a half when I got the feeling that I needed to go to Togo, Africa, and be with my sister.

Once again, I had no idea what I was getting myself into. Starting then, I made a rule that stuck for several years after that: "if it didn't fit in my car, I didn't need it." I wanted to be able to be mobile on a dime.

After a year, my lease was coming to an end in Playa Del Rey. I had saved up a little money and figured I had enough to pay for the trip to Africa and then get back to Cali in a couple of months. My roommates at the time wanted to move on, so I decided to go back home. I had a strong feeling that if I did not travel to see my sister, our relationship would never be the same. How could it be? You have to be in a place like Africa to understand the perspective of someone who has spent three years there. In retrospect, it may have been one of the best decisions of my life.

I was to be home for about three months before I left. My mother needed her house painted, so I was to do that in the meantime. I stayed at my mom's house while I was working. I met a girl at a bar, and I fell in love. A couple of months later and I was smack in the middle of Africa and dying of a broken heart. This broken heart would be my driving force for the next several years. I would be on a mission from that point on to prove I was worthy of great love. Use your broken heart as a tool to take your life to the next level.

Africa was like being on another planet. I was scared to death, and my sister was just totally in control. It was an incredible experience to see my sister being so strong in such a tough place. My little sister is an "old soul" and one of the most courageous people I know or have ever met. She has given her life to serving others and there are too many people to count whose lives she has impacted in a positive way. She served 28 months in the Peace Corps in Togo, at the time the sixth poorest country in the world. She then went on to work as a social worker at a homeless shelter. She worked at Washington's D.C's largest mental agency working with the severely mental ill. Then she got her master's in social work. At this moment in Africa, she became my younger "big sister," and even today I look up to her as someone I admire. That is another story.

I was sitting at an internet cafe located off some sandy dirt road in the middle of Africa. I was trying to send an email to my mom, and as I waited for over twenty or thirty minutes, I finally gave up on the email and had a realization. In the United States, we have high-speed internet. Something you take for granted every day until you do not have it. We have highways, grocery stores, shopping malls, movie theaters, and Walmart.   Africans, particularly Togolese, probably think life in America is like living in paradise. And, I agree, that is probably how it looks, especially when they see images of American TV shows, assuming they have access to a television.

I never realized how lucky I was. My mind exploded. In comparison to some guy in the middle of Africa, my options were considerably larger. I said to myself, What do you want? You can have anything. What is it going to be? You are all out of excuses.

I decided after a few beers with my sister Brittany, in front of her mud hut, that I wanted to be an actor. (Note: No kidding, she was living in the middle of nowhere in a mud hut. Trust me, it is hard to fully understand it until you have been there and seen it with your own eyes. Imagine a small group of mud brick huts with thatched roofs. As you approach, wearing flip flops on a dirt road, a sickly dog walks by as a chicken pecks at a pile of trash that sits out front. The heat is unbearable and you are constantly swiping the flies away with your handkerchief. Your bath is represented by a 50 gallon trash can with a cup floating on top to use to pour on your head. The toilet is a large hole dug into the ground with a make-shift toilet seat on top of a wooden box also known as a latrine. As you sit down on the seat you quickly realize that the things crawling beneath you are roaches, maggots, and flies that will shortly be crawling on you soon if you don't do your business quickly. I would say culture shock would be a vast understatement to this first day at my sister's home in Africa. Needless to say I was shocked to say the least.) Then I said, "And a musician, an artist, a writer, and anything I can dream up to create. I want to make a living being creative. The world is mine." I was so pumped up. Using that inspiration, I wrote the first part of my first screenplay entitled *"Safety First"* by hand in my journal for the next few days after that.

After returning home from Africa, I had a revelation. I knew I was at the beginning of a new perspective. My views of myself, my sister, the world, and life had changed. I had changed.

A few months later, I was back in Texas, flat broke, and living at my mom's house. I had spent all my extra cash on my short-lived love affair. With no money, I was stuck in Texas until I came up with another plan on how to get back to my real life in Cali. I wanted to go back and do it right this time, but I had no idea how I was going to pull it together and make it happen.

Back in Texas, I was at the gym working out when I had a random conversation with another guy who was working out next to me. I told him my story and how I wanted to be an actor and so on. He stopped working out and turned to me. The guy said, "What are you doing about it?" I kinda looked at him dumbfounded, and before I could respond, he said, "Lights, camera—" and of course I said, "Action."

He said, "What action are you taking?"

I said, "I don't know. I mean, I know what I want but I don't know what to do about it."

He said, "TAKE ACTION! Just start doing stuff and you'll figure it out. "

I said, "Doing stuff?"

He said, "Yea, do stuff that is pushing in the direction of where you want to go. Nobody ever knows how to do something until they do it."

He looked at me right in the eyes and said, "You got this."

You can do whatever you want in this world. You can be anyone you want to be. The question is: how are you going to decide on what you want to do, and how are you going to get there? A person can drive themselves insane, trying to answer those questions.

Through all of these experiences, I have realized something. What I want is always changing. As we take action, we start to go in the direction of that desire. As you head in that direction, your perspective changes and that changes what you want.

Don't focus on what you want. Focus on what you're doing about it.

What you want is always a moving target.

What we want is to make it to our goal. We want to exceed all expectations. We want to make it as far as we can go. We do not want to fail. We want to succeed. You never actually get what you want, though, because it always changes, and it is continuously going to keep changing. As you take action and start moving in that direction, you discover more about yourself and the world than you could have ever thought previously. Life has a funny way of teaching you a lesson.

Life is a process-driven art form. In other words, you have to go through the process to get to the art. As an artist who makes process-driven art, I can tell you that, at the beginning of a piece of this style of art, it is impossible to know what the outcome will eventually be. Through the process, the work emerges. As we go through our life, we never know what the eventual outcome will be. But, to get to what we want, it is imperative to go through the process. The other interesting parallel is that what makes art great is subjective. What I think is a successful life may be different from what other people think a successful life is, and what you think will be different as well.

That conversation with my friend earlier was a reminder of the lesson I learned in the past. It seems I still have much to learn. Much of it, I have already learned, and now I am learning it all over again. I have always known the basic idea of what I want. Now, I needed a plan for what I was going to do about it. I sat there, in my recording studio, reminded of that moment with my sister in Africa.

Years later, I was sitting in the middle of my dream. The dream had materialized, but it was all falling apart. It was time to take it to the next level. It was time to take responsibility.

We all are constantly learning lessons over and over and over again. Each time we get better at life and, although none of us ever reach perfection, some of us will reach greatness. Be open and willing to learn and relearn lessons because, as we compile our story and gain more understanding of ourselves, we deepen the meaning of the lessons. As we mess up, fail, fall down, and make mistakes, we get more and more able to avoid those things in the future. But it is a journey. My dad always says: *"You can't be perfect but you can be perfectly yourself."* Don't beat yourself up because you're not perfect, but definitely take a step back and ask yourself, are you learning the lesson?

I decided at that moment that I was the captain of the ship, and I was riding that bad boy come hell or high water. I thought, *If the ship sinks, I am going down with it. I am going to give it everything I have.* I wasn't going to stop until the job was complete. I was going to survive to make it through it. I stood up out of my chair and yelled at the top of my lungs, *"I'm ready, world. Bring it on! I'm ready for my success. I'm not going anywhere!"* I literally did that. I said it out loud.

Say this out loud, *"I'm a_____(insert what you want). I'm in control of my life and my destiny. I'm ready for my success. I'm willing to do whatever it takes."* When you say it out loud, you own it. There is power in owning that you have a choice. You are the captain of the ship. You are the writer of your story.

For those who don't know what they want.

What if you don't know what you want or at least you don't have a really clear picture of what you want? Maybe you are just stuck in a rut and having a hard time deciding what direction you want to go in. I said it earlier, but I want to make this very clear. **Just start doing stuff! Take action!** This works for everybody.

Maybe you have an idea of something that you want to do and so you decide to go for it. You say to yourself "I am going to be the best at this that I can be." You may even become one of the best in the world at some particular thing. Then, one day you say to yourself, "I'm not enjoying this at all, I've got other shit I want to do." Then, guess what? You do something else. Even if you never get to be the best in the world at that thing, at least you will learn a lot.

By the way, being the best at something is a great goal but being good at something and mastering something is the most important thing. Be the best that you can be and realize you are only competing against yourself. But how are you ever going to know if you don't get out there and start doing it? This goes the same way for anything.

You can't focus on what you want because, doing that, you're never going to get there. The worst thing you can do is sit around all day thinking about what you want, doing nothing except thinking about what you want. For example, thinking about money, the most common thing people want, is never going to get you there. You have to go through the process. When I'm running my business, I'm thinking of how to get everything done. There is a certain point when you are an entrepreneur where you have this realization. I'm sure most of you out there who are reading this book who are entrepreneurs are going to understand this. The money is secondary to what you're doing to get the money. If you don't get the job done, then you're never going to get the money. At a certain point, the money isn't even what you're thinking about. You're just thinking about how are you going to get this or that done and making sure it's the best it can be, and guess what? If you do that enough, assuming you own a profitable business, over time you end up with all the money you need and plenty left over.

So, if you don't know what you want, stop using that as an excuse for inaction. You keep telling yourself you don't know what you want, you get depressed, and then you do nothing. Do something, anything, and you will start getting closer to understanding what it is that you want. In other words:

Don't focus on what you want,
Focus on what you're doing about it!

"The journey of 1000 miles begins
with one step." - Confucius

CHAPTER 2

Stop Wanting, Start Having

We all want to be "rockstars". Or at least "rockstars" in our families, at our jobs, and around our friends. Is just being successful good enough? No, we want more. We also want others to view us that way as well. We see this all over the place. From rappers wearing jewelry and sporting fancy cars and houses to billionaires with ridiculous palaces packed with expensive cars nobody ever drives. Look, we all want that, or at least our form of that. There is nothing to feel guilty about wanting to be viewed as successful.

Wanting, however, can be the root of misery. Wanting can be insatiable and like a thirst that never goes away. Understanding this is important because it makes us appreciate the things that we already have in our life. We always want to look outward for satisfaction when true satisfaction lies inside of ourselves.

After much thought on this, I realized that when you stop wanting, you start having. In other words, you find satisfaction with what you already have. One of the pitfalls of getting ahead in life is buying things we think we want when we have an influx of cash and resources, but this always puts us back in the rat race of life. Unless, of course, there is an overabundance or cash and resources. One very big lesson I learned here nearly a year after writing this first paragraph is that when an influx of cash and resources come along, it is important to see them as assets. These assets quickly disappear as we allow our immediate desires to outweigh the bigger picture. There's a big difference between looking successful and being successful.

Just as everything was falling apart and I was trying to figure out everything in the space I had created, bam, it was tax time. I was super stressed out about it because I was worried that I would have to pay taxes. Then, when I found out I did not have to pay taxes, I was relieved until I realized it was because I did not make any money. I was not upset because of the money. I was uncomfortable because I was going to have to go to see my accountant on the other side of town. At the time, I was terrified of going to see him.

More than the dentist even. You know that drill? Yes, worse than that.

I never understood why. He is a nice guy. Why was I so scared of him? It is most likely because I was, at the time, broke and not making any money. Not to mention, I just blew a bunch of cash on what would seem, to an accountant, to be a pipe dream. The accountant was going to hold me accountable.

So, there I was sitting in front of him, the accountant. I let him know what was going on in my life and how I was feeling. Then he said something to me that has stuck with me to this day. He leaned in slowly. He said,

"Zach," making sure he had my attention, "are you listening to me?"

I said "yes," leaning forward to seem more attentive.

He said, "Zach, things don't happen because you want them to."

I crossed my arms and sat back in my chair, confused, even a little insulted. He paused for a moment and said,

"THINGS HAPPEN BECAUSE YOU MAKE THEM HAPPEN!"

I was so relieved at that moment because now I had inspiration. I knew what I had to do. I had to make something happen. Easy, right?

No words have ever been truer than the words my accountant said that day. For me, at the time, it was just what I needed to hear. Things do not happen because you want them to. You can't sit at home all day staring at the wall and expect to be the greatest artist who ever lived. Being an artist is a tough gig. You have to train for years for something like that. It takes hard work and dedication, just like everything else. You have to make it happen, just like everything else. The truth is, if you do not want to work for it, then plan on having nothing.

Now, this goes both ways. You want to be negative and tell yourself nothing is possible? Guess what? You can make that happen. The easiest thing to do is to have a negative "can't do" attitude. I always tell people "if you want to be an artist, you have to get two things out of your mind. "It can't be done," and "it has been done before." It can't be done if you don't try, and almost everything has been done before, so don't let that stop you. I'll talk some more about this later in the book.

I'll take you back to that story in the gym I told a couple of chapters ago. Lights, camera, —

ACTION baby!

In the "microwave" society of today, everything comes so easily and fast. Assuming you have a phone or computer, internet access, and of course, money, you can have anything you want delivered right to your front steps. It has never been easier to get what you want. But that is not good enough. You want more. You want a bigger house, a fancier car, better friends, prettier coworkers. Wait, I am getting off track. The point is everything comes easy, especially if you have money, but what if you don't have very much money? Then what?

I was sitting with my mom years ago, back when I was getting ready to go home from California and then off to Africa. My mother and I were sitting at a little place on Sunset and Pacific Coast Highway, and my mom ordered the trout and eggs special. I will never forget it. I mean, who eats freshwater fish on the beach and with eggs? Just a little extra detail to tell you how vivid the memory is. She just flat out said to me out of the blue, "Zach, I always told you that you can be whatever you want, well I lied."

I was pissed. I said, "What are you talking about Mom? You don't really mean that, right?"

She said, "Yea, I really mean it, you can't be anything you want."

I put my fork down and said, "Yes I can Mom. You just wait, I'll show you."

I took it as a challenge. That is why, months later when I was sitting with my sister in Africa, I decided, *I can be whatever I want, and I will be.* I decided I wanted to be an actor. That is what I really wanted underneath it all. Since I was a small child, I dreamt of being on the big screen. I always wanted to be like James Bond. I even say it today sometimes, "Touchon, Zach Touchon." I know it's cheesy but it's true. "Shaken not stirred."

That was just at the beginning of MySpace. Social media sites like Facebook and Instagram just were not available like they are today. Facebook and Facebook groups had just started, so I was interacting that way the best I could. We still had to print out headshots and resumes back then. In retrospect, it makes me feel good that I started my career in the old school. It was completely different than it is today.

On a side note, while I was writing this section about wanting to be like James Bond, I was out to dinner at my favorite little Italian place in Santa Monica on Montana Avenue. I sat at the bar with my date and got to talking to this old guy at the bar. He was a great guy. We talked for over an hour as he told us some great stories about his life. I thought, to myself, this guy sounds a lot like me.

He was a model, an actor, made music, and loved to write. Then he told us about one of the greatest stories in his life. It was the story of how he got the role and played James Bond. Having our attention, he told us the whole story. I thought to myself, wow, I had just been writing about how I wanted to be like James Bond, and here I was sitting with George Lazenby, the man himself. Talk about the law of attraction.

That night when I talked to the guy at the gym, it dawned on me. He was right. I do need to take action. Back then, I was working out all the time. I was really into the idea of consistent action at the time, and how it leads to compound results. It was very obvious to me, at least the concept anyways. If you want the muscles and the body, you have to go to the gym. Not every once in a while, but all the time. **Consistent action equals compound results**, and if you take a break for too long, you lose the muscle. I will talk a lot about that later on.

I had to take action, and I had to "do stuff" leading in that direction. I had to be consistent and not take breaks, and I had to do it every day.

Still, my mom was right in the end, I can't be whatever I want because I can only be whatever I commit to being. Being whatever you want is a potential, and that potential is limited by all the things you don't want to be and all of the things you don't have the capacity to be. You can be almost anything that you commit yourself to be, but this means sacrificing most other potential opportunities. It is like an arrow: you can shoot it anywhere, even at the moon, but the arrow can only go to one place and that is the target that you point it toward. That trajectory of the arrow toward the target is powered by commitment.

Make a commitment.

I needed a gym. An acting gym, if you will. I knew the only shot I had was on the internet. What I mean by that is, I did not know anybody in the film industry. The problem was I did not have a computer. Today, I can barely remember a time when I was not on the computer all the time. Now my phone is with me everywhere I go, like another limb.

I decided that my mom's house was going to be my "acting gym." I mean, that was the place where I recorded my first two albums, and she had a computer that was working and the internet, so I came up with a plan. I was going to sit on my mom's computer, scouring the internet and sending emails until something happened, anything. It sounded like a great idea, but right away, when I told my mom the plan, she said, "And you are gonna do that every day?" She had a little laugh. That is when it hit me. I needed to commit.

Do it every day.

I decided to stick with the plan. I fell off schedule a couple of times but managed to stay on track. I was working every day possible for two months until I finally got my first audition, a non-paid student film. Woo hoo, right? I was very excited about it. What was I doing? I was sending one email after another most of the time to random people. I was doing anything that I could do that was focused on acting and getting a role.

Stick to it

After I got my first audition, the next came quickly. Then, I finally got an email offering me a role. I thought it was out of the blue until I realized that it was an offer that came from a guy I had sent an email to months before. I did the film. It was great because it was my first independent film, you know with real lights, cameras, and well, you get the point.

There is a residual effect from taking consistent action, sticking to it, and doing it every day; stuff starts to happen. I'm out there hustling, and things are happening. All of a sudden, it can all start happening at once and well, compounding. Suddenly, or so it seems, there you are in the middle of the action.

Don't take a break for too long. Stop talking about it and start being about it. Take consistent action. Do it every day. Remember, every building, no matter how tall, is built one piece at a time.

CHAPTER 3

What's Holding You Back?

Before taking that first step, we need to begin by getting rid of the baggage that is weighing us down. In order to fully understand what is weighing us down, it is important to look at ourselves and take a very detailed inventory. We will begin with what is holding you back. Then, we will focus on what you have and then we will move into the action plan. Imagine our journey to getting what we want. We're packing our bags and, let's be honest, we can't take everything with us. What do we need to leave behind?

So many things hold us back in our lives. When I was going through my inventory and came up with this concept, I realized very quickly that there are various sections. The list includes **people**, **places**, **things**, and **intangibles**. I will go through this list and explain each one in detail, adding some personal stories about what it means to me and what it may mean to you. At the end of the chapter, you are going to make a personal inventory on your "what's holding you back" list.

The hardest part of this section deals with being honest with ourselves because it is far more comfortable to just accept things the way they are. If we want to get what we want, we have to deal with the things that are holding us back. Since you are reading this book, you at least have the desire to get what you want, and that is a good start, but it is time to take the blinders off and look around with new eyes and a fresh perspective.

I break these different sections into categories throughout the book because it's the most logical way to do it. When we break it down like this, it is easier to ultimately see the bigger picture. When things are organized, you have a far clearer view of what is going on and how everything is working together either for us or against us. One of the big lessons here is organization. So, **let's get organized**.

People

People are particularly important because not only can they be the driving force in your life or business, they can also be the thing that is holding you back. Maybe it is their negative attitude or behaviors. Possibly it is financial stress, or the person or persons are just bad people.

When I first started to go through my inventory, I was in the middle of the mess. My business existed, but it was not working, and I was so frustrated. I realized that the pieces were there, but I was having a hard time putting them together in the right way. Knowing that waiting on my partners' film productions to come together was not working. So, I started to look for other options. Of course, at the top of my people list was my partner, who was slowly becoming my ex-girlfriend.

People who are a negative influence on your life do the following. They tell you that you aren't good enough. They say you'll never make it. They may be abusive towards you. Maybe they are always yelling at you and making you feel bad about yourself. They might want you to join them in their negative behavior patterns. They may be talking you into doing something bad, wrong, or illegal. They may always offer you drugs and alcohol as a solution to your problems. They may beat you down with their words telling you that you're fat or ugly or stupid. They may be out of harmony with you and your environment. Maybe they are always asking for favors and money, but they never want to give anything back in return. Maybe they won't pay their bills and now you don't have any electricity, wi-fi, gas, water, or a place to stay. Maybe they are stealing from you. They could be your spouse or partner and you know they are messing around on you, and maybe even be putting your body in danger by doing so. They may be telling other people things about you behind your back. They may be misrepresenting you or telling others secrets you told them in confidence. The list goes on and on. If I missed one, write it down.

You need to identify a problematic person first. You need to see them for what they are and acknowledge that they are not good for you. When you do this, it becomes nearly impossible to not add them to your what's holding you back list.

Write it down and remember, this is for your eyes only; you don't have to share this with anybody.

Places

Places can carry so much baggage. Maybe it is a lease or a mortgage that is difficult to get out of. Maybe your mom lives right down the street and this does not let you spread your wings, or your kids and ex-spouse live in the same city. Maybe it's the neighborhood you grew up in and it is continuously reminding you of who you have always been. Whatever the reason, it is hard to be honest about whether the place you are in is what is holding you back. Just to be clear, I am not recommending walking away from all of your responsibilities. What I am suggesting is analyzing your current situation in the effort of finding clarity.

In my case, when I came up with this concept, I was stuck in a lease that I couldn't afford and it was going to be difficult to get out of. There were homeless people all around and although the area was gentrifying, it wasn't happening fast enough. There was trash everywhere and the graffiti was a never-ending problem. Being street level, I was always dealing with safety issues that were hard to ignore. In addition, the product I was selling wasn't the best thing to be selling in this area. I looked around and I could clearly see that the place I was in was holding me back.

Years before, I was living in my hometown. I had so many dreams, but I felt trapped in an environment that didn't support my dreams. I was always reminded of who I had always been. My perspective was so small looking back and I knew that I was never going to get what I wanted being where I was. So, I packed up and moved to Los Angeles.

Maybe you are staying at a house and in that house bad things are happening. You keep telling yourself that there is no other option, so you just stick around. Eventually, this environment will affect your life; there is just no way around it. Maybe your business is a great business, but it's just in the wrong location. You may be living in a bad neighborhood because you're stuck in a mortgage or lease agreement and so you just keep your family there. Now your kids are being influenced by their environment and it could have devastating and potentially irreversible results. There are far too many to list, so put some thought into this and, if I didn't describe your situation, write it down so you can look at it. I will discuss some more later in the book but, if you think the place you are in is holding you back, **_write it down_**, this will be great later when it is time to reflect.

Things

The next area on the list is things or what some may call "stuff." These are physical things like an old couch, a junk drawer, all the items in your garage, an old tv, and anything you can see around you.

I had so many things, from furniture to art to sound equipment, clothes, tools, and a lot of "useful" junk. I kept saying to myself, the second I throw this away, I am going to need it. Just watch. So, I just kept holding on to things. I was out of places to tuck it all away, and I needed to take action. I needed to differentiate the things that were adding value to my objective from the things that were weighing me down and keeping me from moving forward.

In this section, I recommend that you **take a hard look at the things around you** that are there but serving no purpose or possibly even holding you back. We all have this in our lives. Assuming you are not a nomad with one bag, you are probably like me: you have so much stuff, you don't know where to put it all. In my case, the worst thing about it was that most of the things I had acquired were free or at least a good deal.

The things that are holding you back are usually obvious, and you know they are just taking up space, but they don't just take up physical space; they take up space in your mind and are doing their part to keep you from your goal. Maybe there are things that you haven't even seen for potentially years, but yet that box needs to be there, staying there until you are dead. Wait a second, let's take the time to define the purpose of the stuff. If you can't find a purpose, then these things can go on your list. ***Write them down.*** We'll do something about it in the following chapters.

Intangibles

What exactly are intangibles?

Intangibles could be positive or negative, but for the sake of staying on track, we are going to talk about the negatives first, and then we will move on to the positives later.

I added intangibles to the list because there are a lot of unseen things that could be holding you back. An addiction, bad habits, bad time management, or even a bad attitude can be holding you back. You have to be overly honest with yourself until it hurts enough to recognize these.

Another area of intangibles that could be holding you back is a lack of education, training, or know-how. This book is a great start, but I want to encourage you to never stop learning. Feed your mind as much as possible and always educate yourself because what could be holding you back could be your unwillingness to accept that you don't know everything and, in order to get what you want, you might need more information. Arrogance is another intangible as well, so be humble and start with being willing to change if necessary. With that being said, keep one thing in mind. We are what we eat, essentially, so feed your mind and your body positive things that ultimately lead to you getting what you want. If you are feeding your mind negative information, feeding your body poison, and feeding your environment with junk and bad people, the outcome will be a result of those things, a crowded life surrounded by the wrong people, a sick body, and a negative mind and attitude. Keep this in mind because another intangible is the unwillingness to accept that certain things are bad for us.

At the end of my inventory, I came to a conclusion. I needed to stop blaming everybody else for my problems. The fact is that it is my fault. I can take steps to change my situation. I have the power, but only if I am honest with myself and am willing to take full responsibility. The other thing is that I need to be the student and the teacher in my own life all at the same time. I need to be open to accepting that I can continuously grow, and when I am "hitting a brick wall," so to speak, I need to learn to let go. I need to stop putting possibilities in cages and trapping them in old beliefs.

I was doing my first runway show as a clothing designer. I had all of the clothes and all of the models. I was busy helping organize the event simultaneously, so I didn't have time to think about who was wearing what. The director came up to me and said, "Hey Zach, you are up next. Fifteen minutes." I freaked out because I had no plan. I was running around in circles, trying to figure it out. I said, "Somebody hand me a pen and paper." When I got everything down on paper and had a plan, all of a sudden, I calmed down and relaxed, knowing that I had it under control. That is why it is crucial to see it on paper. Most of the time, the biggest intangible is the lack of a solid, organized plan.

Are there intangibles in your life that are holding you back? ***Write them down.***

Luck has a way of finding you.

I am standing in Marina del Rey looking out at the marina while waiting to spend the day hanging out on a yacht with some friends. I am having a moment of gratitude, and here we are on intangibles. Wow! That is a tough one. I got stumped when I came to this chapter. Right away, I realized something. You see, when I came up with the idea for this book, I did my inventory just like you are doing right now. Now, I'm writing it, and I realized that there are still a few things on my list that I haven't taken care of. What a perspective change. The realization that there is still so much work to do. Personal work. The little ugly monsters in the closet that need to be taken out and looked at.

Just a little side note: as I am writing this, a guy walks up to me and asks, "Frank?"

I looked up from my phone and said, "No, but I played Frank in a movie. I was Frank for a few weeks. That's funny."

He says, "Are you still doing any acting?"

I say, "yea I got one coming out in a few months."

He says, "Are you looking for new management?"

I say, "I'm always interested in new management. What do you have in mind?"

He says, "My dad is a partner of one of the biggest management companies around. You want me to give him your number?"

I am not saying that some big break can or would happen in this situation, but it just goes to show that when you are on your path,

luck has a way of finding you.

*"**Chance favors the prepared mind**."* – Louis Pasteur

CHAPTER 4

What Do You Actually Have?

Now that we have started to look around with a new perspective, it is time to take an inventory of what is around and inside of you. What people, places, things, or intangibles have value or contribute to you getting what you want and where you want to be? It is so easy to take the things around us for granted and, usually, most people let the things around them just sit there and collect dust. Things that can be helpful to you getting what you want are easily holding you back at the same time because they are taking up space in your life and your mind instead of being used to help you get to your goal. Now it is time to focus on what you have.

If you google the word "asset," you will find the simple definition is that an asset is a useful or valuable thing, person, or quality. That is what we are looking for. What do you have that can make you money, be sold and make you money, or benefit you in some way? I discovered many times that what you gain from an asset is not always money, so keep an open mind. There are lots of other ways people, places, things, and intangibles can benefit you. All around you are ways to create value. Let's take a deeper look into what I am getting at. At the end of the chapter, there will be a "what do you have list," so feel free to take a break and write down what you have if something comes to mind.

People

Like I said before, people are the most significant factor in your life or your organization, and they are usually your biggest asset. People have qualities and skills that can benefit you, they have contacts and advice you need, and they can perform tasks for you.

My dad always told me that the things that are most important in life are time and energy. Everything takes time and energy. The key to getting what you want is to take advantage of the time and energy that other people can contribute. Teams work so well because more people equal more accomplished. But you have to be willing to work with others and stop trying to do everything by yourself. After all, your time and energy are limited.

"Lost Time is never found again." - Benjamin Franklin

All businesses are relationship businesses. People are the reason you do pretty much anything. Somebody has to buy what you are selling, right? Someone has to live in the house that you are building. Someone has to drink the tequila that you are making. You get the picture.

I was all alone in the construction process of my gallery and studio, which was quickly becoming something else. I was so overwhelmed, and I just wanted to give up. So, I started to look at my assets. There wasn't a lot of money, so I began to get creative.

I have always had a lot of friends, but I never looked at the people in my life as assets. Not in a negative way. More in a very positive way of taking advantage of the skills and contacts that people around you have, and finding a way to benefit from what they are capable of contributing. With that being said, you have to accept that you are also an asset for them. Find out what you can do for them, so they will do what you need them to do for you. Relationships are built on reciprocation. So, be sure to understand that you are not trying to get something without giving anything in return. It is an exchange and this exchange strengthens ties.

Right away, I realized I had to be willing to ask for help. I had to admit to myself that there is no way that I can do everything myself. Although I felt superhuman, my very human body was slowly showing evidence of fatigue.

I have a memory of my dad saying to me as a child, "you can learn everything about a man from the way he cleans the floor." He doesn't remember telling me this at all. I found it very interesting how we can put so much thought into something that someone else doesn't even remember saying to you. That gave me perspective.

I always took this to mean that the floor had to be perfect. So, I would clean the entire four thousand-square-foot space on my hands and knees. For some reason, I had to have it perfect. It was madness. I took a step back one day, threw down my rag, and said, "I am going to go buy a mop." You see, I realized something, it does say a lot about a man. I cared about the task I was performing, I paid attention to detail, I created a system, and I followed through by finishing. But I needed to have the right tools to do the job, especially keeping time and energy in mind. Then, I had to let someone else perform tasks, and I had to accept that it is not going to be perfect all the time.

Cleaning the floors drove it home. I needed help, and I needed it badly. Worst-case scenario, I could do the task again, but odds were, eventually the job was going to be just fine with someone else doing it.

One thing you might discover, as I did, is that someone or multiple people who are on your "what do you have list" may also be on your "what's holding you back list." That is a clue to what I will talk about later.

The truth is, I wasn't all alone. I had people all around me who could help. It was pretty clear that I was having trouble communicating with those around me and letting them know what I needed. Once I made myself available, I even got help from complete strangers. People who needed something from me and were willing to, in return, give me something I needed. Not all of it was money. Much of life is bartering with others; trading with one another is a key component to getting what you want. Think outside of the box. Remember, the benefit of an asset is not always money, but it can be a contributing factor. So, let your mind think of those around you as assets and ***write their names down.***

Places

Yes, places can be assets. The property you own is an asset. In addition, your business location, the house you own, your neighborhood, your job location, the city you live in, the church you go to, and on and on, can all benefit you. When you start wrapping your mind around seeing places as assets, you will get it. The home you own has value. The business you own should be an asset. The church you go to contains contacts, clients, advice—all of these can benefit you. What places can be assets to you? **Write them down**. Remember, people and things exist in a place.

Things

What do I mean by things? The things we are focused on are physical things that have value or can benefit you and propel you towards your goal. You can hold them, touch them, see them, and use them. A painter has brushes. A software guy has a computer. Tools of the trade are a great example of a thing that can benefit you. But that only scratches the surface. Get creative when looking at the things around you and you will begin to see that the things around you may hold more value than you realize.

I got lucky when my good friend donated some great things. His old office was downsizing, and he had to get rid of stuff fast. So, of course, like a kid in a candy shop, I took everything he would give me. I had no idea what some of it was, but I thought, hey, maybe I could get something for it.

Suddenly, my gallery was packed. Although most of it was good stuff, there was just so much of it stuffed into every crevice that every drawer and corner was overflowing with stuff. The things started to affect the business as they leaked out of the storage. I had to create new storage to pack in all of the various items. Combined with my partner's assortment of things, it was just out of control.

I realized I had been procrastinating with the projector. It was old school, but worked great. I wanted to start doing film screenings. That is the moment when it hit me, what other stuff am I not using?

Things are always going out of date nowadays. So, the best time to utilize those things is right now. Take a look at the things you have and see which ones are assets. **Write them down.** In other words, they bring us money or value or can benefit us in some way, and it is not always in making money.

Intangibles

At the moment I was creating the idea for this book, I was sitting in the middle of the mess, and all I had was *time* and *energy*. All the money was gone, and I was close to falling off the edge. That is when I looked deeper. That is when I wrote down one of the intangibles: *drive.* Drive can be defined as the innate, biologically determined urge to attain a goal or satisfy a need.

A while back, I was competing in a mud running contest with my cousin in Texas. There is a reason why it is called a Mud Run. You have to crawl through the mud, then, while wet and muddy, continue to the end of the race. It is brutal, or at least this one was. My team was lagging, so another guy and I pushed the other two guys to pick up the pace. Later on, my cousin, who was one of my team members, said, "That's why I put you on the team, you got drive, man. It's like when that little voice says give up, you're done, you just keep on going."

The drive inside you is a perfect example of an intangible asset. It is something you have that benefits you directly when you employ it. Charisma, good looks, bad looks, a specific skill, a trade, talent, know-how, expertise, bravery, and the list goes on.

Look at yourself as an asset because you benefit yourself. You are your greatest asset. You have qualities in you that can help you get what you want. But you have to use them and be in full control. I said bad looks on the list. I wrote this because it is an excellent example of how a bad intangible asset can be a good thing. Think about a strange-looking actor who has used that to rise to fame and wealth and respect.

Recognize who you are. Be honest with yourself. Accept yourself. Look at your surroundings with new eyes and **write down** some of the intangible qualities that you have that can help you get what you want.

Assets change in value as you change your perspective.

CHAPTER 5

Ignore, Remove, Improve

Ok, you know what you want, at least for now. You know what you have. You know what is holding you back. You want to take action, but what are you gonna do about it?

In this chapter, I'm going to talk about a concept I came up with called "**ignore, remove, improve**." We are going to start with what's holding you back. Take a moment to look at that list again. Don't worry, it's not set in stone, and you can keep adding to it.

Back to the first time I moved to Los Angeles. I was living with actors in Playa Del Rey, sleeping in a closet and figuring things out. One of the guys I was living with was a very close friend of mine from Texas named Danny. He was young, I think twenty-one at the time, so needless to say, he was messy. I would tell him over and over again, as I furiously cleaned up after him, "clean house, clean mind!"

If you want to get something going, the first thing you need to do is clean house. Like I said before, those things aren't just taking up space in your space, they are taking up space in your mind and your life.

When I decided to move to LA the first time, I sold everything I owned and made a rule. If it doesn't fit in my car, then I don't need it. Now, I know that is extreme and it works for a young single guy with no kids on a mission to "blow up." But essentially, it's true. One of my favorite singers, Erykah Badu, has a song called "Bag Lady." In this song, she tells a story about a woman she names Bag Lady and lets her know that she will "hurt her back" by carrying all of the bags she lugs around. She goes on to explain that all you need is yourself. It's a really great story about not letting the baggage of your past weigh you down. It's true, baggage weighs you down and not only metaphorically.

People

People on your "what's holding you back" list are very hard to face. Why is this? It's because it's emotional. Maybe you love the person or people, but they are not good for you. Maybe you have some kind of deep need to be loyal to someone who doesn't return the favor. Maybe you are related to them or they are an old friend who you share so many memories with. Whatever the reason, it is difficult because if we face the fact that they are on our "what's holding you back" list, then we know that we will have to do something about it and all the emotional baggage really makes that tough to do. What I found right away is that people on my "what's holding you back" list were also on my "what do you have" list. That's what led me to the idea of ignore, remove, or improve.

What are you going to do about it?

You've got the first option, **ignore**. Ignoring a person in your life isn't always easy. This is different from remove in the sense that you don't remove them from your life, but you just ignore them and do what you can to keep them from affecting you. Not the easiest thing to do, let's say, if they are your boss, your guardian, a coworker, your spouse, or even your business partner. In this case, you need to focus on **you**. Don't go to the same place after work as they do. Change your routine, and do what you can to ignore them by focusing on yourself.

In my case, I was in business with a partner who was also my girl-friend, and we were in and out of living together. On top of it all, she was known as someone who is impossible to ignore. I tried to ignore her, but she would command my attention, usually in the form of an argument. She was a lawyer and that's what she was good at, arguing. I was on a mission at that point and on the verge of going broke. I refused to give up or give in. I was relentless in my pursuit of making something happen. I wasn't going to let anything or anyone stop me.

That leads me to "**remove**."

I had to remove her from the space in order to save the business and, of course, my own ass. But we didn't break up. I would just keep working around the clock and be too tired to talk too much when I got home or, should I say, to her new place. You see, I never moved any of my stuff into her new place. I was already separating myself mentally, but that was the beginning of the physical separation. Of course, it was just going to get worse, but I had a lot on the line and

I needed to make something work. I saw it as protecting her and me from complete disaster. My heart was in the right place.

I was aware that she was on my "what's holding you back" list, but she was also on my "what I've got" list. It was a tough situation. She meant the best, I think at the root, but we just kept bumping heads. We had a discussion and we both agreed we needed to make something happen. It was a tough time for both of us. But we decided to keep pushing.

At this point, we were working on a script for a client of hers. We worked on it for about six months. The script was done and we needed to sell it. We only had the next month's rent and no action going whatsoever. The space was starting to work, but it wasn't making enough money yet. So, we worked on making a deal.

To make a long story short, we ended up selling the script and made some good money. The final product was one hundred and sixty-five pages and was based on a true story, so it required research and multiple interviews and meetings. But it turned out great and we sold it.

All of the sudden, we were back in the game. But for how long? Would I be able to pull something together?

This is a perfect example of how flexible the strategy of ignore, remove, improve is. It works as three options to deal with someone who is holding you back. You can do any one of them or, in my case, all of them. Ignore them while you remove them, then improve what you can to squeeze the most out of the situation.

Eventually, if you can't improve a relationship with someone on your "what's holding you back" list, and that someone is impossible to ignore, then inevitably if you want to move forward with your life and get what you want, they will have to be removed.

I made my first "company policy" around that time. I decided that *"any relationships that are not reciprocal will be terminated immediately."* I decided that I don't have time for people who didn't contribute to me getting where I want to go. So, in other words, as the old saying goes, "if you're not with me, you're against me." As it turns out, my partner was totally against me and was doing all types of things to hold me back. But in the midst of our relationship, I was too blind to see it. I found out the following year that she was actually telling everyone that she owned the place and she just let me hang art there. Needless to say, I felt like such a fool in the end. But I also finally felt that I indeed had done the right thing.

Let me say this clearly, if someone is abusing you or bullying you, misrepresenting you, disrespecting you in front of others, spreading manipulative lies behind your back, or holding you back in a toxic way, you must and have a duty to remove them from your life. Stop wanting a better situation and create it. Don't wait. Do it now. It starts with recognizing it. It may take some time, but you can get through it. Don't allow the people on your "what's holding you back" list to drag you down and make you fail; take action and responsibility and be relentless.

Places

Places are also tough to deal with. For example, you may be like I was and stuck in a lease or mortgage, or you may have to stay put because of your family or your job. Or you may have no money or car. All of these are tough circumstances about a place, but action can still be taken.

Ignoring where you are is unproductive and something that poverty thinkers do. For example, the more poverty, the more trash, the more a property is ignored and falling apart, the more roaches and rats move in, and it just perpetuates. As the trash builds up, it gets harder and harder to clean up. Eventually, the poverty-minded people just ignore it.

There is a saying in the hood. "I can't have nothin' nice." If you grew up in a bad neighborhood like I did, you would know exactly what I'm talking about. You hear this all the time. The light switch doesn't work, "man, I can't have nothin' nice." The car is falling apart, "can't have nothin' nice." The yard needs to be taken care of, "can't have nothin' nice," and so on and so on.

People in the hood are not lazy. That's not what I am saying, they are just infected with a very common case of poverty thinking.

Poverty thinking is infectious and relentless. It helps to create a false reality where the average person is powerless over their environment and generally unable to change their circumstances.

In a stand-up comedy special, Dave Chappelle tells a story about his childhood in which he says, "Dad, I hate being fucking poor." He goes on to say, "And my dad got really upset." His dad says to him, "David, David, David. We are not poor. Poor is a mentality that very few people ever recover from. Don't you forget it, son, you are broke. Broke is temporary."

People become complacent. In other words, we accept that things suck and just ignore it. As the mess piles up, we get so lost in it that we then give up and just live with it. Not only do we live with it, we spread it and infect others around us with poverty thinking with the very innocent sounding phrase: "Man, I can't have nothin' nice."

Let me be very clear about something, the "poverty mindset" is not exclusive to the poor; it is a mindset that occurs almost regardless of one's financial situation. There was a time in my life when I had poverty thinking. I still struggle from time to time with the symptoms. I grew up surrounded by poor people and I was constantly being influenced by everyone around me. Everyday my belief that "there was no way out of the hood" was reinforced by the people surrounding me who all said. "it's so hard to make the bills," and that they could, "never get out of the hood." Thinking about the bills I used to complain about blows my mind because they were so small in comparison to my new perspective now, and I am sure that the bills I complain about now will be very small in future when my perspective is even bigger.

People say that they are stuck in the hood, but that is bull shit. It's completely untrue. You can remove yourself from your environment and start fresh somewhere else. You can educate yourself and pull yourself out of poverty thinking. You have the power to move. If your life depends on it, which it could, get the hell out now.

If removing yourself from a place isn't possible right now, you can **improve**. Fix the broken stuff. Clean the house. Clean the car. Paint the house. Mow the yard. Pick up the trash. There are some amazing stories about people who have changed their home, business, and even communities with very little money, but it's not easy and takes a different perspective and a lot of hard work. So start small. Why is the world going to bless you with more stuff when you can't even take care of the stuff you have? Where are you going to put all of the new stuff if your place is packed with old stuff? Do you think any of your new successful friends are going to want to hang out with your old friends? Food for thought.

If you want to remove it, make a plan and start taking action. If you want to improve, stop procrastinating and start right now! Whatever you do, don't ignore it. Unless, of course, you're ok with being a poverty thinker. Remember "clean house, clean mind."

Just a quick side story to the moment I realized I was infected with poverty thinking. I was complaining to my godfather about my life. About how hard it was and all the stuff I had been through. He stopped me mid-sentence and he said to me, "Zach, would you stop doing that? I mean just stop telling people about that. It makes you look bad. How about you keep it simple and just say, I come from humble beginnings."

In my case, I was in a commercial lease and I couldn't get out of it. By the way, if you're thinking of signing a commercial lease just be aware that it is very difficult to get out of. Just keep that in mind. Anyways, I obviously couldn't just ignore it, I couldn't remove it, so I was forced to improve it even more. Remember, I had already spent a bunch of money renovating it. When I say a bunch, I mean everything I had.

The space wasn't working as a studio, at least one that makes money. My partner had quit and I was in a position where I had to make something happen, anything. We will get to what I did in the next chapter.

Things

Things hold value or they don't. They contribute to your life or they take up space and even keep you from getting what you want. Let's look at the things on your what's holding you back list.

Remember you have three options. First, you can **ignore** it, which is usually what most people do. Here's what I did to ignore. I built a storage room. Remember, I was hung up on letting stuff go, but that was quickly changing. As I ran out of storage, I had to prioritize and the things that were unnecessary and taking up space had to go.

You can do a number of things with things holding you back. You can improve them and use them, assuming they can be improved. You can also improve them and sell them. In this case, it's a win because now you are taking something that is taking up space in your mind and your life and using them to make some money which you can then use.

The last thing is to remove them by giving them away and throwing them out and hopefully selling them. In my case it was a mix. But what I realized was that the stuff that I could sell, I couldn't really get much for, so I just threw them out and gave them away. I even put a pile and a sign that read "free stuff." It was pretty amazing because when I did this, I realized there were other people that could use the stuff that I didn't want. They were grateful to have the stuff and it felt great. Remember sometimes what you get isn't money, sometimes it's a good feeling. In this way, you just turned something holding you back into something that benefited you by making you feel good and you may even start a new relationship. You can also donate them to charities and write it off. There are so many ways to benefit others with the stuff that's crowding your life.

Intangibles

Intangibles require that you take a really honest look in the mirror and it can be really tough to face. They may be addiction, laziness, complacency, and a ton of other intangible qualities that are holding you back. You can't ignore them; you can improve them, but that's always temporary. Ultimately, these bad qualities have to be removed. It takes hard work, dedication, and being very real with yourself. You have to focus on this every day and make it happen. If you have an addiction and especially a bad addiction like one to drugs or alcohol, remember there is a lot of help out there. Reach out and take action to remove that from your life. By the way, you will free up more time in your life to build a network of new "people assets" that will help you overcome and, hence, move you toward your goals.

Just a quick story that happened while I was writing this book that really shows the power of being on the path. This happened as I was thinking about the idea for poverty thinking.

I was working on a beautiful home overlooking Los Angeles right off Mulholland Drive. And how did that happen? I was painting another house in the Palisades when suddenly this guy pulled up and said, "Hey, are you the painter?" It was serendipity because it was while I was thinking up an idea for being open, being ready, and being willing to say yes.

I had been on the site for a day and the electrician was there before me. Apparently, he had been there a while. I was trying to get the job done as quickly as possible, so I was a little annoyed by him because he wanted to talk. Finally, I took off my headphones and I listened to him.

He started to go on and on about negativity.

"It's so hard, man. You know, working all the time. Right?" I looked at him and said, "Hey, I'm just grateful to be working." He said, "Yea, but being away from your family. It's hard, right?"

I said, "You know what, man, what are you getting at? You got kids?"

And he said, "No, I just, you know, it's hard, that's all."

He just went on and on until I just had to let him know about poverty thinking and how it's a sickness.

I said, "Listen, man. You are conditioning yourself to be miserable. You are reinforcing the idea that it is so hard. You are talking yourself into it. Every time you tell yourself a negative thought you create another brick to build a negative reality. Your whole dialogue is filled with negative affirmations. Now you have to create a new reality with positive thoughts and words and actions."

These negative affirmations create a drag on your life. It takes twice as much energy to do your daily tasks if you are resisting your life.

Then, I told him the story about my godfather and to say you come from humble beginnings. So, he finally stopped talking to me for a little while, while we worked.

Then, out of the blue, he said "You are one smart guy. You can have anything in this world that you want."

I stood up and turned around to him and said, "You know what's great about that statement you just made?"

He just looked at me until I said, *"That works for you too, man, you can be anything you want, but the big question is: what are you doing about it?"*

He went on to tell me that he had a drinking problem and was reaching out. The stuff I said really got in his head. I'm not saying I changed the guy's life or anything, but I am sure that I planted a seed.

Planting seeds of negative thinking with statements and actions, you create your negative reality. You have to give yourself positive affirmations to create a positive reality. Through the use of practice, your perspective changes and a new reality emerges.

In any given situation, you can have a positive attitude or a negative attitude. Your choice. That is totally up to you. A little secret; a positive attitude is always the right choice no matter the circumstances. I'll talk some more about this later on.

It dawned on me at that moment that I might be onto something here. Maybe there are other people that the ideas in this book can help. Being inspired about what you are doing is very valuable as it pushes you to dig deeper. Being your own source of inspiration is crucial to make it through some of the more trying times of any big project. Find inspiration in what you are doing.

Remember, there are three ways to deal with the things on your what's holding you back list. You can ignore them, improve them, or remove them, and sometimes all at the same time. Take a look at that list, take a hard look at it, and remember you have the power to do something about it.

Clean house, clean mind.

CHAPTER 6

Utilize, Visualize, Realize

What good is something that's useful and can help you get what you want if it's not being used? The best time to use something is right now. In this chapter, we are going to talk about a concept I came up with called **utilize, visualize, realize**. I'll first describe the concept and then break it down into categories on your "what do I have" list.

Utilize

If you Google the word *"utilize,"* you'll find the definition is: *"make practical and effective use of."* The synonyms are awesome and right to the point of what we are talking about. For example: *into service, press into service, take advantage of, exploit, milk, tap, turn to account, bring into play, bring into effective action, and deploy.* It's a really powerful word and right on the mark.

Inside you, outside of you, and all around you are things that need to be utilized. These things have to be utilized by you or someone you employ or instruct. The two key words in the definition are *practical* and *effective*.

Practical: *of or concerned with the actual doing or use of something rather than with theory and ideas.*

Effective: *successful in producing a desired or intended result.*

Ultimately, you have to actually do something or use something, rather than depending on theory and ideas, and be successful in producing the desired or intended result.

You have to Take Action. To utilize means to actually use something and be successful in letting it benefit you. The best time to utilize is now; it always will be.

There is also the fact that a thing is useless until the right moment to use it. For example, a hammer is only useful at the moment that you need to drive a nail. A needle is only useful at the moment that you need to sew something, and so on. A lot of things are about timing and circumstance in order to achieve maximal utility. So, keep those tools in your toolbox so they are ready when the time comes.

Visualize

If you Google the word *"visualize,"* you will find the definition is: *"to form a mental vision or to make something visible to the eye."* The word visualize is a verb or an action word.

This is the next step. Now that you know you can utilize, you have to form a mental vision and then make it visible to the eye. Basically, you come up with a strategy of how you are going to utilize something. You have to see it, in your mind. You have to have an idea of how to utilize it. You have to have a plan. Then you Realize.

Realize

If you google the word *"realize,"* you'll come up with four definitions:

1. Become fully aware of or to understand clearly.

2. Cause something to happen.

3. Give actual form to.

4. Make money from a transaction.

In other words, you gotta make it real. So just to put it all together.

We have to actually do something or use something rather than dreaming about it, and be successful in producing the desired or intended result. We have to have a plan and fully understand what we want and then cause something to happen, actually do it, and make money or benefit from it.

So that's the concept. Now how do you put it into action?

Let's take a look at your "what do I have" list. This was exciting because now I understood that I had something. Which is a whole lot better than I felt when I thought I had nothing. Hopefully, you feel the same way. If not, let's keep digging.

Places

Let's start with **places**. In my case, I was in a great place. I was in downtown Los Angeles with a four-thousand-square-foot gallery studio right in the fashion district. It came to me when I was making my inventory. I have my location, that's valuable. It definitely sounded cool, anyway: "art gallery, downtown LA." Yea, there were the homeless and the graffiti and the trash, but I was in Los Angeles. I thought to myself, *if I can make it here, I can make it anywhere.*

It hit me, the fashion district. I should take advantage of that. I should design some clothes and set up a fashion store. I knew that I could find everything I needed around me, plus I had a lot of paint and art supplies. I knew that I had style, so I thought, ok, let's put that on the list of possibilities.

After my partner decided that she didn't want to be a part of it anymore, I went from paying half to all of the rent and it was really adding pressure. The script income was running out fast and I had to do something. So, I made a decision that I was going to focus on doing events by renting the space.

Simultaneously, I was going to launch a fashion line of men's custom clothes. You see, also on my list was the fact that I was a great painter. I was already making art. At the same time, I would put out the word that I was looking for curators to do regular shows. I also set up a punk night with live music to pick up momentum. In the meantime, I scoured the earth for people to get involved.

Here's how it happened. I was complaining to my godfather again. It was one of the last times I did, since I was snapping out of my poverty thinking. I said, "Nobody cares about art. Nobody will buy my art, nobody cares. I don't know what I'm gonna do. How do I make them care?"

Of course, he disagreed and said, "I care about art."

And I said, "I know, but you already bought one."

We had a laugh and, later the next day, I decided I was going to make art on clothes. The idea was that people only care about themselves, so if I paint on clothes and make people feel cool, then it's a win-win. I already had a good presence as an artist on social media, but I was having a hard time coming up with interesting ways to incorporate art. So, I put art on the clothes.

In other words, I combined strengths. I knew how to utilize my talent, so I applied it in a new way with the brand: "Art of Wear."

A week later, I was walking to my gallery, which was on the brink of becoming a clothing store, and I saw a guy doing a photoshoot. He was a good-looking kid. I was in the process of making clothes at that time, so we were working on the top floor. The space was a clothing factory. Clothing hanging all around the room, drying. Mannequins in the corner sporting the day's ideas. It was street level with huge windows. I said, "Hey, you guys can shoot over here in front of my art, it would be cool."

Next thing you knew, we were doing a photo shoot with my clothes. It went great. The kid, Andrew Noah, and I have become very close. I even put him in my first fashion show, which really kick-started his runway career. Today, he's designing clothes and living the dream as a model working in the fashion industry. Eventually, I would realize that he was wise beyond his years.

At the same time, I was making music. Lots of it. Every day. I was also good at music and producing. We had a recording studio set up for doing voice-overs for all the films that we never produced, so naturally we started to make music. One of the musicians I had brought on board was a kid named Van Vegas.

I saw something in him. He needed a place to stay, and we were working on his first album, so he started crashing with me at the studio. He was to become a great friend to me.

The point is that I embraced where I was at. I looked at the place and saw what the location could do for me. That's taking a place and utilizing it, visualizing what you're going to do with it, and making it real. Before I knew it, I had lots of bookings and then began to pick up selling clothes.

Things

Things take on a momentum of their own. You decide on a direction and see which way it goes, then keep rethinking it until it goes somewhere or not. Are you gonna get rich and famous? Who knows?

It's better to try and fail than never try at all. It's even better to try and succeed.

People

That leads us to people. People are at the root of everything you're doing. Business is based on relationships and people are at the center of that. People can really be the key factor to help you make or break an objective. Not just at work or with money or other activities, but with family, friendships, and other relationships as well. Everyone around you can benefit you in some way and most of them want to, so the key is understanding how they can be of value to you and how you can be of value to them.

With business and personal relationships, the benefit can be very obvious and simple, while in other ways complex and difficult. Sometimes it's monetary and, at other times, it's a feeling you get from them or even the offer of a place to stay. In many ways, there can be a degree of flexibility because there are lots of people, until you rely on someone. Then it gets tricky because although there are a lot of people, not a lot of people can be relied upon. The people on your "what do you have" list are your biggest asset and they need to be treated respectfully and taken seriously. Whatever you do, don't take advantage of or manipulate these people because that is sure to end a perfectly good relationship.

Being honest with yourself about people is always difficult. With people comes a host of different types of baggage, but mostly feelings. In relationships, you base a lot on feelings that you may have for those people, and although those feelings can be good or bad, they can definitely be misleading. You need to find out if these people on your list are actually benefiting you.

I needed people around me. I needed to distance myself from my relationship that was growing ever more toxic by the moment. Luckily, I had Van and Andrew there with me to help with the shop and the transition. After another argument, our relationship came to an end. Although we had just "officially" broken up, we had really been broken up for over eight months.

Momentum began to pick up. I was still dead broke, but I was scraping by and keeping it together. After a month or so, I was to have a meeting with another group of people who wanted to do an art show. I had done a classical concert with a Russian musician who I really liked and he assured me that the people were very cool.

One afternoon, I was in the middle of a day selling clothes with Andrew. Van was downstairs making music. I was finally starting to feel like myself again and things were starting to come together.

Intangibles

This is a huge one and, in fact, the whole book could be about this topic. Although we are just going to scrape the surface on this, I'm sure that you will be putting a lot of thought into it. What are the intangibles? Your gifts, the things that you are good at, the abilities you have, your talents, your know-how, your education, your possibilities, and anything that you can use to get what you want that you can't see, touch, and feel. We all have these special qualities and unseen things that we can use, but some of us take them for granted, not even realizing they are gifts, or we don't know how to capitalize on our strengths. Don't let them go to waist.

What are you good at and how are you going to put that into practical use? Look at the things that you are good at and really enjoy doing, and find a way that you can put that to use in a practical way to make you money or push you towards your ultimate goal. **Where we spend our time is where we find our success.** So, make sure that you are focusing your energy on something that, at the very least, doesn't make you miserable.

Visualize how you are going to put your talents, strengths, assets, attributes, intangible qualities and so on into action. Literally see it in your mind. See yourself already where you want to be, using your intangibles. Then, realize this by making a plan and taking action by benefiting from it or making money from it.

People who are good with people may go into sales or customer service, but that same quality can be used in public speaking or starting a podcast, for example. In my case, I am a great painter and I love making art, but that can also be applied to painting houses, painting on clothes, and whatever else you can imagine. What I realized after painting houses for a long time was something very interesting. One day, I said to one of my workers, "You know, I am a pretty good painter, but you know what my real business is? It's people, what I'm really good at is people. What I'm really good at is sales; painting just happens to be what I'm selling."

You see, you can take one intangible asset and literally sell it using your other intangible asset, working with people. When you open your mind to this, you start noticing it all the time. So, write down your intangible assets and put together an action plan on how you are going to put those assets to work for you.

Just to sum it up, use the people, places, things, and intangibles on your "what do you have" list as tools to get what you want. Visualize where you want to be and how what you have can help you get there. Then, realize your goal by making a doable step-by-step plan and taking action. Then, repeat this process until you have reached your destination.

CHAPTER 7

Ask for Help and Focus

on What's Working

I had been single for a while, and was sure that I would be single for a very long time. I was recording a song called "Broken Faith" just before a meeting with art curators. That's when I met Katerina, who was curating the show. A beautiful Russian girl with black hair and blue eyes. It was like a fresh breeze just came into the gallery and blew me away.

Right then, I knew that I may have met someone special. We began to work together on the project and, after a few weeks, began to fall for one another. By the time the art show opened, we were officially in a relationship. Things were changing and they were changing fast.

Something had changed about me over the past couple years in my previous relationship. Not only was I in the middle of being myself, one hundred percent, I was also doing what I loved and beginning to get my feet on the ground. I had learned to be more decisive and I came to a place where I knew what I wanted in a relationship. So, when I met the girl of my dreams, I didn't hesitate one bit.

Suddenly, I felt joy for the first time in the nearly three years since my mom had died. Although it was a ways off, I could see the light at the end of the tunnel. My priorities were quickly changing, but I wasn't out of the weeds quite yet. There was still much work to do. Falling in love in the middle of a disaster isn't always a bad idea.

The show was a huge success. Loads of people showed up and Katerina did an amazing job. I was blown away with her ability to connect with others and be organized, and just the general business side of her was very impressive. I knew then that this relationship had the potential to go way beyond just a romantic one.

How was I going to start a new relationship and give the time and commitment that that takes while I had so much going on with my business, not to mention everything was falling apart and one disaster could destroy what little I had going. I only had one thing that I could do: ask for help. I was falling in love, and fast, and I knew that somehow, there was going to have to be two of me. I needed to have someone managing the store, someone managing the events, and someone building a relationship all at the same time.

I knew that I had to be the one building the relationship, obviously, but I didn't have to be the other two. At this point, the only person left was Van and so I had to ask him for help. I hated asking him for help because, in my mind, I thought I was supposed to be helping him with his career. How could I ask him to help me? Not to mention, I was dead broke and couldn't pay him very much.

I asked him if he could help out and of course he agreed. He didn't mind at all; as a matter of fact, he told me it made him feel good seeing me happy for the first time since we had met. He said that he thought that me being with Katerina was a great idea and he would do whatever he had to do to support it.

Focus on what's working

The momentum started to build at the gallery as the event side of the business picked up quickly. It was a brutal process because we had to set up the clothing store, then break it down and do the event. Then clean and set up the store again the next day. We did it over and over again. The process was very difficult and the truth was that keeping the clothing store going just wasn't making any sense.

We decided to pack up the clothes and stay focused on the events which were actually getting us close to making rent. It wasn't an easy decision, although it was obvious. I loved making clothes and being a designer, but I had to focus on what was actually working, not what I wanted to work. Sometimes that's one of the hardest things to do, being real with yourself about what is actually working.

I'm not saying scrap ideas altogether, but if something is taking a lot of time and energy and isn't giving back, you should think about putting it on the back burner. Don't forget that what's holding you back is usually you and your desires for what you want, and your ego has a lot to do with that. I had to ask myself, what was more important? Was my relationship more important than trying to keep pushing the clothes that were breaking even but not really working? I decided that the relationship was more important, so I transferred the time the clothes were taking up to Katerina.

Now, there only had to be two of me, and it was looking more and more doable for me to get this relationship off the ground. Falling in love is awesome. One thing about falling in love is that it really brings a lot of stuff to light. The most important of those in my case were two parts, money and a place to live.

You see, I was crashing at the gallery with Van and that wasn't going to work, at least not for long. Her lease was coming to an end and I knew that we needed to get a place together, but how was I going to do that with fifty bucks in the bank? Although it was soon to be moving in together, I didn't feel like it was too soon. I knew what I wanted and this time I wasn't going to let fear hold me back. I decided I was going to try to take the relationship to the next level. So, I asked Katerina how she felt about it and she was so excited to say that she was definitely interested in looking at some places.

We decided one afternoon to go out looking for an apartment. After looking around at a few places, nothing really caught our eye. When we got to the place I thought we would really like, the front desk person was rude to us and we decided to give it a break. On the way back from there, we were headed back to the gallery and decided to check out the place across the street from the gallery, but they said they couldn't show us a place for a few days. We were a little bummed, but just figured it wasn't the right time, so we went back to the gallery.

Then we decided to go grab a bite to eat and, as we passed by the window in the building where the basketball courts were, suddenly a basketball slammed against the window. We both turned towards the window and noticed it was TJ, one of my good friends who happened to live in the complex. I waved to him to come let us in. When he got to the door, I explained that we had been wanting to check out the apartments and asked if he could give us a tour. He said, "I can do better than that, I know the guy who can give you a real tour, a guy named Christian."

TJ walked us over to the office and got us a meeting and a tour with him that day. Not only were we given a tour, we were now friends of friends. Long story short, we ended up getting a great deal on the top floor apartment that overlooked the nine thousand square foot mural I had done, and the gallery was across the street from that. We took it as a sign that we were definitely in the right place.

That day, I got a call to do a paint job and, in just a couple of days, I was able to come up with all the money. That's when I was reminded that: "Oh, yeah, I'm a painter." A perfect example that **while you are walking your path, luck has a way of finding you**. We moved in the following week, just in time for her mom, who was visiting from Russia. We were so excited to be able to show her mother the beautiful apartment.

Then I got another call for a very large paint job, which led to another and, once again, we were on top of the game and things were going well. The gallery was going great, the art shows were happening, we were booked every week, and I was in love. What could go wrong?

CHAPTER 8

Make Personal Changes

When I got to the last part of chapter seven, I came to a screeching halt. Who am I to write this book? What kind of hypocrite am I? I'm writing this book and I still have so much on my "what's holding me back" list. I felt unqualified to keep working on the book before I really looked at my list and dealt with it. Not to mention, someone else was counting on me.

The questions I kept asking myself was, am I worthy of her love? Am I going to step up to the plate and become the man that I always wanted to be and the man that this beautiful woman was going to want to love and deserve? Do I deserve success if I am not willing to do the hard work and have the discipline to follow through and stick to it? Should I even finish the book if I'm not willing to practice what I preach?

I took a few weeks to really meditate on it until I found myself standing in a hotel in Santa Fe. This was a moment of deep mourning because the reason Katerina and I were there was for a funeral. We were there to support my little sister Nisa, who was having a hard time after losing her boyfriend just a few days earlier. He was a local musician and I was coming to discover that he was actually a legend there and all over Albuquerque. His name was WakeSelf and he was one of the greatest rappers that ever came out of the Southwest. He was killed by a drunk driver and his life and career were cut short, and my sister was left to pick up the pieces.

In this moment of reflection, I realized that I had to accept responsibility and make some personal changes. I also realized that as human beings, we are flawed, we are not perfect, and the pursuit of being great is a constantly refreshing cycle. In other words, don't become paralyzed because you're having trouble making personal changes.

Remember clean house, clean mind? This is also true with the body and lifestyle. Are there habits and lifestyle choices that are on your "what's holding you back" list? Should there be?

The hardest part about making personal changes is admitting that there is a problem and something is holding you back. Maybe it's alcohol, cigarettes, eating habits, sexual habits, drugs, and the list goes on and on and on. Bad addiction and habits are not only success killers, they can also be cold-blooded killers as well.

In my case, I had been smoking since my mom passed. Then more people passed, my stress level was always at full blast, and I came up with one excuse after another. If you are doing something because it's a choice, look deeply at your decisions. If it's an addiction, admit there is a problem and take steps to do something about it.

Remember the reason that I am writing this book? I wanted to make my life better, and smoking cigarettes had to go. The truth is, until I got to this part in the book, I was still smoking. I wasn't going to keep writing until I had quit smoking. Then, I quit smoking and I did it cold turkey. Although it's been some time since I stopped, it is always a battle. It takes hard work. It takes changing your daily routines and habits that lead to you doing other bad habits. It takes owning that there is a problem. You see, I didn't want to write this in this book because I am totally embarrassed to have been a smoker. I am embarrassed that I was addicted. I am ashamed that I couldn't make the decision to quit for so long. Now, with someone counting on me and hopefully a family in the future, I really want to be healthy and alive for them. I had to come to the decision that it was time, and then quitting wasn't so hard. Like the old saying goes, one day at a time.

Habits are the key to getting what you want, but not bad habits. Bad habits are called bad habits because they are not good for you or the people around you. Your bad habits don't affect only you, they also affect everyone around you, like your family, friends, coworkers, and even complete strangers. These effects can be devastating and can have long-lasting impacts and, in some cases, can lead to prison and death. Bad habits are serious business, although at first they seem innocuous and innocent.

If you search bad habits on Wikipedia, you'll get this explanation: "A bad habit is a negative behavior pattern. Common examples include: procrastination, overspending, stereotyping, nail- biting, and spending too much time watching television or using a computer." Not all bad habits, however, are so innocent.

Bad habits have to be broken and they can only be broken by you. You have to break the bad habits and begin to build good habits. I'll talk about that in the next couple of chapters. Notice that they mentioned procrastination. In other words, doing nothing or waiting to do something for too long is also a bad habit. If you want to quit smoking and you keep putting it off, the real bad habit that you might have besides addiction to nicotine is procrastination.

The thing about bad habits is that, in some cases, they can lead to addiction. Addiction is the next level where you can't stop the bad habit. In this case, many times, you need help to break the addiction and won't be able to do it yourself. If you think you are having a problem with addiction, you have to do something about it now. Don't wait until it is too late.

"Search others for their virtues, thyself for thy vices." - Benjamin Franklin, *Poor Richard's Almanack, 1738*

Bad Habit = Bad Outcome
Good Habit = Good Outcome

Adjust your attitude.

I was with my family in St. Louis for the holidays one year when my grandfather Ed Heck was still alive. There I was with a negative attitude after a few too many drinks, complaining about my childhood. I was starting to argue with my family, in hindsight for no reason except my own selfishness. That's when my grandfather slammed his hand down on the table and said, "Boy, it sounds like you need an attitude adjustment." Of course, that stopped me in my tracks.

Positive Attitude = Positive Outcome
Negative Attitude = Negative Outcome

I did need an attitude adjustment. Most of the time when we are getting negative and complaining about the past or present, we need to take a step back and adjust our attitude.

A negative attitude is a goal destroyer. The old saying comes to mind, *"you attract a lot more bees with honey."* In other words, your attitude attracts the same attitude, so negative attracts negative and positive attracts positive.

Attract the positive with a positive outlook and attitude; don't be your own goal destroyer.

Create your own history.

I touched a little on this in an earlier chapter when my godfather told me to say that I came from "humble beginnings." It is true that all kinds of negative traits can run in your blood or are passed through DNA. There has been a lot of research on this and it is true. In other words, some people are more predisposed to addiction and other bad traits than others. But, with that being said, don't use this as an excuse.

My mother was a great woman. She raised four kids who all went to college. She worked sixty to eighty hours a week to do it, but she never made me feel like a burden. But it wasn't always like that. She was a victim of sexual abuse, a drug addict, an alcoholic, and she had a host of things that could have defined her, but she had the strength to overcome those the best she could.

In the end, she died twenty-three years clean and sober and I am so very proud of her for that. She is a shining example of someone who overcame her addictions, bad habits, and history, and was able to get what she wanted, a healthy, happy life. That took a lot of hard work, drive, a positive attitude, and she had to constantly renew her vow to herself and her family every day. She also was a member of several twelve-step programs, particularly Alcoholics Anonymous, which helped her keep her vow to herself and her family. I am eternally grateful for her friends in AA, without whom she would have never made it as far as she did.

It's true that our life history helps to create who we are today, but it does not have to control us or define our character tomorrow. I have had to stop using my past as an excuse to make bad decisions now. Use your past and learn from it. If necessary, recreate it.

What do I mean by that? Take out the negative shit from your mind. Focus on the positive stuff and don't allow the negative in, and when it does creep in, acknowledge it and let it go.

What we speak is what we are and we manifest everything into existence by speaking it into reality.

Don't speak about the negative. Don't allow the negative to control you and hold you back.

Where you are doesn't define you. Who you were doesn't define you. The stuff crowding your life doesn't define you.

You define you!

CHAPTER 9

Building Successful Habits

Now that we have identified the bad habits and have made the effort to make those personal changes we have been ignoring, we need to replace them with positive habits. Positive habits are the key to building a life that can support you getting where you want to be and having the things that you want in your life. **Positive habits are most powerful when put into action.**

Give a shit.

Pardon my French, but I think using the "bad word" really drives home the point that I am trying to make. The first step to being successful is giving a shit. If you don't give a shit then you don't give shit, and if you don't give shit then you don't get shit.

You have to care. You have to care about your clients, friends, family, and team. You have to care about doing a good job. You have to care about getting what you want. You have to have pride in what you are doing or you don't care enough to do the job right.

When you really care about something, you find a way to make it happen. When you find yourself procrastinating, you can look at the thing that you are holding off on doing, and if you're honest with yourself, you will probably find that you just don't give a shit.

What happens when you do care? You do a great job. You improve yourself. You get repeat business. You have better relationships. When you care about something you have pride and take owner-ship. When you achieve the goal that you care about, you find fulfillment.

In reality, if you don't give a shit, then what's the point? If you are doing something that you don't give a shit about, then find something you do care about and do that. Unless you don't give a shit that you won't ever get what you want. Let's face it, you have to give a shit to get the shit you want.

Avoid saying "I" too much.

When you are dealing with people, avoid saying "I" too much. I always say, "My dream isn't a 'Me Dream,' it's a 'We Dream.'" In my dream, everybody that is on my team, in my family, and every-one that is a part of my life and ambitions is successful, thriving, and fulfilled.

Being a leader means that you care about your team, objectives, family, and so forth, more than you care about yourself. Leaders find fulfillment in helping others get to their goals as well. Remember, relationships are built on reciprocation. To get something, you should give something. If you are taking and not giving, the relationship won't last very long and, ultimately, the other party will probably have resentments. The best deals are the ones where everyone wins.

Be the leader you want to follow. Go for it and don't need a pat on the back. Nobody is going to pat you on the back for doing something for yourself. People only pat you on the back when you do something for them. *"Congratulations, you just won the championship,"* your team member says. *"Now I'm a champion."* Be the leader that pushes for a win for everyone and you will get your cherished pats on the back. Leaders bring victory to the entire team and beyond. Leadership is understanding that you aren't doing it for yourself, you are doing it for the team. Be the one who leads the team to a victory and you are the leader. Being a leader means you care about the goal of the team before your own well-being, so it is important to prepare for this and treat yourself well now so that you are prepared to suffer through the tribulations that bring your team to victory in the future.

The old saying comes to mind, "There is no I in TEAM." When you are just doing things for yourself and your ego is taking over, all of the sudden you start saying "I" all the time. That makes others feel like they are just there to make your dreams come true. You have to say, *"Look what we accomplished,"* or *"I know we can do this."* If you watch any interview of any great champion, they always say, "I didn't do it alone, I wouldn't be here without my team and none of us would be here without the fans." Which leads to the next good habit.

Give credit when credit is due.

Never take all the credit for everyone else's accomplishments. When someone does something that benefits the team, organization, or family, it's important to recognize it.

We all know that being a professional artist is a tough gig, like most creative things. The reason is that it's hard to sell art. So, how does the artist who is not making a living at it keep making art? If an artist isn't making any money, what is the artist living for besides self-expression and the love of it? The artist is living to be noticed and appreciated.

I can tell you as an artist that money is secondary to being appreciated as an artist and having others enjoy the work. It is encouraging. People love to feel like they matter. It's amazing how far people will go if they feel like they are appreciated and what they are doing really matters. So, part of motivating others is making them feel appreciated and that they matter. Make them feel like you notice them and that the work they do makes a difference and plays a part in the achievements of the group as a whole.

Be the first one there and the last one to leave.

I was at an event on the Westside and got to talking to a man who was at the event about success and getting there. He told me his story. He started by saying,

"You know the saying that ninety percent of success is showing up. Well, it's true. Let me tell you, Zach, I worked towards my success for my whole life and I didn't really start getting to the real money until I was fifty. You know what I did? I showed up and I just kept showing up. Eventually, success will find you and you know where it will find you? It will find you working. Success never finds people who don't show up because they aren't there when success arrives, someone else is."

This man was very wealthy and about sixty-five years old. I won't say who he was, but when I say wealthy, I mean a multi multimillionaire. So, I would say he is an authority on the subject. It took him until fifty to get his first million and, by sixty-five, he would have over fifty million. How did he do it? He showed up.

But he didn't just show up. He was the first one there and the last one to leave. He would always push harder than everyone else. He was the leader of his company and, to be the leader, you have to be there to lead.

So, if you want success, ask yourself, are you the first one there and the last to leave? The one who sees the whole project to the end has a greater chance to reach the next level. It shows initiative being there on time and first and it shows follow-through by being the last one to leave. Just keep this in mind.

Always go above and beyond.

The easiest thing to do is "just enough"; that's what people who are ok with being mediocre are all about. When you do just enough, you are being average and being average is not the right aspiration. The average person doesn't care enough about what they are doing to go above and beyond. When you are dealing with clients, teammates, family members, and others, you have to put in the extra effort to get the full benefit of a relationship. People are used to others doing just enough, so when you go above and beyond, you stand out as someone who is worth investing in with more time, money, effort, love, attention, resources, and admiration.

You never hear anybody say; "I really admire that guy, he is so average. That guy only does just enough. Wow, I want to be just like him."

I started my first business when I was thirteen. It was a landscaping business. By fourteen, I worked up to having over forty yards that I mowed and took care of. I had a mower that I pushed and I pulled a little red wagon behind me sometimes up to over a mile radius. I was walking to a yard to go mow when a man stopped. He was impressed and asked me if I ever thought about doing handyman work.

I told him that I didn't have any business in the winter months, so I would be willing to work with him when the landscaping season came to an end. John, my first mentor, would make a major difference in my life. He drove home the idea of going above and beyond. He said every job you do, always try to find something to do that is extra and don't charge the client for the extras. I saw the result firsthand and very quickly became convinced as I watched him develop relationships with his clients.

By going above and beyond, clients would dig to find other things for us to do. Things they may not necessarily have thought of before. They enjoyed giving us work and felt great when they handed him money.

People feel good about contributing to you, your life, and your goals when they see you going above and beyond. They feel like you deserve to be treated with respect and paid what you earn because you stand out as someone special.

This philosophy has been my secret weapon that I always employ. This philosophy is how I have been able to achieve so much. The people in your life are the reason you have success. By going above and beyond, you give them a reason to feel proud to be associated with you. If you begin to make it a habit to always try to go above and beyond, you will find the result to be more love, respect, work, money, and fulfillment than you can ever imagine.

Always finish.

The hardest part of any race is the last lap. In high school, I ran the mile and did really well with it. I held the number one spot for a while, and I can tell you that the last lap is the deciding lap of any race and it is the most difficult one. When you are coming around the last lap you have paced yourself and trained yourself to know that you have to now turn it up a notch as the guy behind you slowly catches up. You have to give it everything you've got to, as my coach would say, "*finish strong*."

We have all seen the last person at a marathon. The one for whom this may be the greatest challenge that they have ever faced. Everyone cheers them on as they slowly make their way to the finish line. When they finally cross, although they are dead last and the marathon has already ended, everyone is inspired as they break down from exhaustion.

It's inspiring to see someone finish a race when all odds are stacked up against them. If the last person just gives up, then everyone is disappointed and the person feels terrible. People are inspired by individuals who overcome their shortcomings and find their own victory.

Inspire others by finishing strong. Worst-case scenario, you can walk across the finish line, but if you finish, you will find that now you have a new sense of accomplishment that pushes you to finish even stronger the next time. If you just quit, then you are conditioning yourself to be mediocre.

When things are left undone, everything before means nothing without getting the job to the finish line. Don't leave things unfinished due to procrastination and making excuses. Make it a habit to finish everything you start. Whatever you start, big or small, finish it.

When you do someone a favor, don't remind them about it all the time.

I remember the first time I learned this lesson. I was just a kid and my dad was all pissed off. My grandmother had given us a dishwasher and every time we saw her, she would remind us about it. Remember when I did this or that for you. The natural response is, "Yea, and...what's your point?" The other person would respond by saying, "Oh I don't know why that came up, I just wanted to say it. How's it working?"

When someone does this, in this case my grandmother doing it to my dad, it makes the person that received the favor feel resentful and sometimes, in my dad's case, mad. I remember him saying, "Why does she always do that? When you give something, you should always give from a place where you expect nothing in return. Except, of course, gratitude. There is a limit to the gratitude you should expect."

When you remind someone of what you did for them over and over again, it usually leads to the person never asking for a favor again. It really is a relationship killer. Next time you try to do a favor or give someone a gift, they will be more and more hesitant to receive anything from you. The worst kind of situation like this is when it is someone who really needed the favor. Then the person uses the "gift" as a way to make the other person feel less than or even expect all types of favors. If you are on either side of the coin, remember when doing favors for others, don't keep reminding them, and if you're the receiver, be careful about who you let do favors for you and what you are really receiving.

Always plan.

The old saying by Benjamin Franklin comes to mind ***"If you fail to plan, then you are planning to fail."*** There is a reason I mention this so much. It needs to be driven home. They didn't make that saying up for no reason. It sounds obvious, but it is actually the main reason people fail to get what they want. Like I said, I talk about this again and again, but it is worth repeating over and over. Always plan.

Be like water.

Water changes as its environment changes. It can turn solid if it freezes. It can be hot or cold. It can even turn into gas and float away. Water is unstoppable, and one of the most destructive and most creative forces. Look at the Grand Canyon and you can tell that when water wants to go somewhere, it will find a way to get there and, if you stand in its way, eventually it will win.

To be like water in this case means that you have to be relentless, you have to know where you are going, you have to never give up, you have to change when it is necessary, and you have to adapt to your environment. Know when to freeze and when to boil and know when to float away and move to the next place. Rain down on the world with your success and make a big splash when you do it. Be like water and nothing can stop you.

Always leave on a good note.

This is one of the hardest things to do. When there is an argument or disagreement, when someone screws you over, or when you just had your worst failure, leaving on a good note can be very difficult. What you want to do is say, *"Screw it, I'm out of here,"* throw up your middle finger, and leave. What you want to do is leave the place a complete disaster and let somebody else deal with it. What you want to do is stick somebody else with the bill and run away. But you need to take a second to understand what happens when you do that. You burn bridges, you create bad impressions, and you make enemies. This can really come back and bite you later. What can happen is way worse than sucking it up and doing the right thing.

It takes humility and hard work, but if that is your forte, eventually it will be your reputation. Eventually, there will be a time that opportunity will find you because your reputation is that of a person who always does the right thing and leaves on a good note.

Take the high road.

When things were getting really bad at the gallery and I was about to lose everything, loads of "opportunities" were coming up, none of them good. They all were the "low road" type or opportunities that would eventually lead to a bad place.

I was walking down the street one day praying and thinking about what to do. I said, *"God, I need to know what to do. I am about to take an opportunity that could lead in the wrong direction. I know that it may be a little risky, but at this point I don't know what to do. I'm thinking about doing it. What should I do?"* Suddenly, I was overwhelmed with the feeling, ***"Be Patient."***

I knew what I had to do. Take the high road. Do the right thing and be patient. I had to accept that if things were going to fall apart, then that's what was meant to be. Things can get a lot worse than just bad and taking the low road can lead way beyond just bad. I knew that it would mean more work, but eventually it would be worth it. Just a couple of weeks later, I met the woman who would become my wife. Be patient and take the high road even when it's not the easy thing to do.

"The time is always right to do what is right." - Martin Luther King

Take all meetings.

How are you going to know what can happen in a meeting if you never take a meeting? When you want to get something going, it is important to take all meetings. All kinds of things can come out of a meeting.

You can learn something you didn't know, you can find opportunities you didn't know existed, you can find new people to work with, you can create new ideas, you can learn something about yourself, you can make something happen that you never would have known about, or worst-case scenario, you can eliminate another person from your list.

If you don't take a meeting, what can happen is you miss opportunities, you learn nothing, you're still the same old you, and you leave yourself thinking, *"Should I have taken that meeting?"* People like to make excuses that they are too busy to take meetings and that they are too successful to take meetings with certain people, and although these both could be true, they are not true when you are starting out. There is nothing worse than looking back with regret thinking, *"Man, I should have taken that meeting, I wonder what could have happened?"* The worst thing that can happen is that you don't take a meeting and the next thing you know, you are looking at the guy you didn't meet enjoying his huge success while you keep refusing to take meetings. Take all meetings so that when you look back, you can say hey, at least I listened to what the guy or girl had to say. Don't be so big headed when you start off that you close yourself off to opportunity.

Take responsibility for everything.

I said it earlier, but I am going to say it again. If you want to be the boss, you need to take responsibility for everything. That means when something goes wrong, you are to blame. When somebody on your team messes up, look at it from the perspective of, *"What could I have done better? What could I have done to prevent this from happening?"* If you can't find an answer to that, then ask yourself, *"What can I do to make sure this doesn't happen again?"*

When something goes wrong in a company or a country, who gets the great majority of the blame? The president, the leader, the person at the top does. Why is that? Because if you are a good leader, then you have to take full responsibility for everything. If you don't want to be the one to blame when something goes wrong, then just give up now and go follow somebody. But if you want to lead, then you need to step up to the plate and be the leader that accepts the responsibility.

When you are wrong, promptly admit it.

Have you ever busted somebody messing up? They make excuses and start to try to lie their way out of it. They come up with all kinds of reasons to justify why they messed up. Don't be that guy. Be the person who stands up and says, "Yea, I messed up, but I apologize and I'll try to be better."

We all make mistakes. We all run late to work or meetings.

We all mess up sometimes. Try to find the solution instead of compounding the problem by lying and making excuses. Tell the truth and admit it when you are wrong. If you truly care about being successful, you will find ways to improve and you will be wrong less and less.

Your head can't be in the clouds when your feet need to be on the ground.

Being an artist and creative person in general, I can tell you that this has been one of my biggest hurdles. It is easy to have your head in the clouds, meaning painting a painting, writing a book, making music, and doing all kinds of stuff that you are passionate about and could eventually lead to your success, but this, at the moment, isn't bringing you any money. What you should be doing is figuring out how to get some income going so that you can pay the rent, electricity, and keep food in the fridge. If you have a family or someone who is counting on you, this is particularly important.

I can create around the clock. I can paint all day, make music all night, shoot videos, you name it. When it comes to creating, I can just keep going nonstop. But there has to be a balance between that and making money. If that makes you money, then great. Stop creating in the "clouds" and take a moment to get your "feet on the ground" to finish a project and get paid. If you aren't getting paid to do your dream, then you need to get your head out of the "clouds" and get your "feet on the ground" and get your ass to work. Bills come first. If you need to create full time, then it needs to be somewhere and in a situation where you aren't paying for anything and no one is counting on you. There are situations where creating full time can work, but that is in a situation where the money is coming in or someone else is taking care of that part.

Remove "it can't be done" and "it's been done before" from your vocabulary.

This works for all people who want to do something new, but for the sake of telling a personal story, I will relate this to creative people. When I meet a new artist that I am helping out or when someone asks me for advice, one of the first things I tell them is to remove "it can't be done" and "it's been done before" from your vocabulary. The reason is obvious and very simple; **it can be done** and **everything has been done before**. Well, almost everything.

For example, you are writing a song and your buddy keeps saying, "I've heard that before," or "Hey, that sounds like *[blank]*." Then you become discouraged and stop writing the song and it never gets done. This same thing happens with all endeavors. Another example is when you are trying something new and someone keeps saying, "That can't be done," or "That's not possible," and the same thing happens, the idea dies.

If you have someone in your life like that, then put them on the "People" section of your "What's holding you back" list. If you are the little voice on your own shoulder, train yourself to shut off that part. Stop letting ideas die because you think that it's been done or it can't be done. Most of the best ideas in the world are just a combination of things that have been done before. Everything that exists in this world at one time couldn't be done. There are too many examples to mention here, but let's be honest, did anyone ever think country music and hip hop could be combined, today it's a whole new genre. So, push through the negative thinking or find some new friends to sing to. Remember, it can be done and it will be done. The question is, is it going to be done by you or somebody else?

Stick to the facts

It is easy to get wrapped up in lies and hype and start weaving a web of your own lies. You can keep yourself out of trouble by sticking to the facts. We all know the story, one lie leads to another and then another and then another. Those lies become impossible to keep up with and, before you know it, you are busted.

This can end your career, relationships, and kill deals. In a lot of places, this is actually illegal and when you lie badly enough, it can lead you to huge fines and even prison. Don't try to make something out to be more than it is; it won't work out. There is no better game than just being blatantly honest. A lot of times, it catches people off guard because they are so used to people lying. But that leads us to our next habit…

Don't be too honest.

I'll keep it simple on this one. Basically, don't tell people things and be honest about things that they may not need to know. Try to keep yourself from ruining people's opinions of you because you are too honest about things that you shouldn't be. This doesn't mean lying about things, it just means don't tell things that don't need to be told. This doesn't mean hiding pertinent facts or details about a deal that need to be disclosed.

Here's an example. You are in the middle of a sales meeting and your client asks, "Where are you from?" Then you answer, "I'm from Texas." Then they say, "Oh yea what part?" and you say "Southside Fort Worth, in the hood. You know the crack head side of town where all the gangsters live. I grew up with drug addicts and prostitutes walking down the street. I knew what guns, sex, and cocaine were before I could multiply." Then the client leaves totally freaked out and you wonder, "*What did I do?*" Don't be too honest.

Push yourself to do more than you think you can do.

We all put limitations on ourselves. We all think we can only do so much and never push ourselves to do more. As a matter of fact, what we like to do is lie to ourselves and say, "*I'm giving it all that I've got.*"

The truth is, until you are forced to push yourself to the limit, then you don't know if you are giving it all that you've got. How do you force yourself to go further? By putting yourself in situations that are bigger, better, and more complicated and harder to do than anything that you have done before. Make a bigger commitment than you have in the past and what you will find is that you had no idea what your limits were. What you will find is that you are tougher, stronger, smarter, and just better in general than you can imagine now. Push yourself to make bigger goals and commitments. In other words...

always tell yourself you can deliver even if you have no idea how you are going to deliver.

Don't talk, communicate. Don't hear, listen.

It is really easy to kill a deal by talking your client into the dirt. Guess what? It's always true, not just in business. Everybody's favorite subject is themselves and everyone's favorite voice is their own. Take advantage of this by being a good listener. When you are listening, take notes in your mind and make eye contact. Try to stay focused and stop thinking about what you are going to say next, and think about what question you are going to ask next. The better listener you are, the better communicator you are, and the more you will get out of conversations. This might be the most powerful habit of all.

Score, score, score, then score some more.

One of the most common mistakes that I have made is that when I have a big score like a movie, a big paint job, or selling a script, or any influx of cash, I have always had a bad habit of chilling out. I would say, "Hey, I'm good. I'm just going to relax now. No rush." But, of course, before you know it, the money is running out, bills are due, and what happens? You freak out and start from the beginning all over again. I've done it time and time again.

What I've realized is that when you score, you need to keep scoring, and then after that, score some more. What I mean by this is pretty simple and straightforward: keep stuff in the pipeline. If you get a big payday or a major successful moment happens, take that and use it as momentum to jump into the next thing. Once you are in the next thing, then take a little break while you are pacing yourself. As that next thing is coming to an end, get some other scores scheduled.

Never spend the money before the check clears.

You really want to kill a deal? Start talking about how much money you are going to get and even start to spend the money in advance. The second something goes wrong, you are smack in the middle of a complete crisis. By behaving in a way that the money is on the way, you could potentially make deals where you can't hold up your end of the bargain and then kill the relationship. Always be honest with yourself. Is the money in the bank?

CHAPTER 10

Immediate Action

Now that you have worked on your lists and you know what you need to do, it's time to take immediate action. Procrastination leads to doing nothing or doing the right thing too late. Talking about doing something takes the same amount of energy, if not more, than actually doing something. How many times have you thought about going to the gym or heard somebody talking about how they are going to work out, but they never actually do?

Our mind is our greatest asset, but it can also be our worst enemy. Lack of planning is a bad thing, but overplanning leads to finding reasons to not take action. When you think about accomplishing something too often, something bigger, better, and more complicated than you have done in the past, you will find yourself saying *"I can't do this."* You'll say that *"there's not enough money, manpower, supplies, the time isn't right,"* or some other excuse.

We have all had the experience, most of us as kids and maybe even now in your life, when you're lost in the mess. You're standing in the middle of the literal mess surrounding you in your bedroom. Your mother, father, or spouse wants your room/house clean and you are old enough to do it yourself. You feel overwhelmed and you say, *"I don't know where to start.*" You begin cleaning, but you're just moving things around. Where do you start?

You start with the trash. The stuff that obviously has no worth to you; it's not serving a purpose in your life, or its only purpose is to crowd your space and your mind and weigh you down. Once you remove the trash, then you can begin to organize the stuff that is useful to you. After organizing, you begin to clean by putting things away where you can find them. Then you reorganize while you detail clean. Cleaning house really is a metaphor for life and that's a major part of what this book is about.

I remember when I learned this lesson. I must have been about nine years old or so. I had been telling my dad for days or maybe even weeks that I would clean my room, but still hadn't done it. He would tell me over and over again until finally he got mad at me and said, "Do it now. Don't come out of your room until the room is clean."

There I was, locked in the mess. I looked around, and it was so overwhelming. I mean, it was a disaster. That's when I went to my dad and said, "Dad, I don't know where to start."

I was so frustrated. He said, "Figure it out," and went back to whatever he was doing.

After whining about it for a while like kids do, I started cleaning my room. At first, of course, I was frustrated and made a bigger mess running around in circles and throwing things around. Then I tried to give up, but my dad wouldn't let me. Then I was finally at the breaking point where I had no choice but to clean my room. I had no idea where to start. After procrastinating a while, I decided to dive in. I made my bed. That's the thing when you are lost in the mess; you start somewhere that will make an immediate impact and give you a starting point. In a bedroom, making the bed gives the feeling of accomplishment right away. But it is only the beginning, especially in my case at nine, where my room was a disaster. After making my bed, I put everything on my bed and I started figuring it out. I started with the trash and then went through the process I described earlier. I remember thinking, I'm going to figure out the fastest way to clean my room. It took hours and hours.

Finally, I had the room put together and I went back to my dad. I said, "Dad, I did it. I cleaned my room. Aren't you proud of me?" I stood there with a smile on my face, I felt so proud. He ignored me. I said, "Dad? I cleaned..."

That's where he cut me off. He turned directly toward me and said, "Do you want me to congratulate you?"

I said, "Yea, I did what you told me."

He said, "I'm not going to pat you on the back for doing something you should have already done. I'll pat you on the back and say good job when you cleaned your room without having to be told." I didn't understand. I stood there dumbfounded. He said, "You have to get things done, you have to do it without somebody having to tell you to do it, and you have to get it right the first time."

I was disappointed at first, but the point really hit home as the years went by. It's a great life lesson in leadership because, eventually, there is no one to tell you to clean your room and, if you want a clean house and a clean mind, you are going to have to do it yourself. You're going to have to do it without being told. You're going to have to do it immediately. You might not get it right the first time, but eventually you get there. **The most important thing is to do it now! Don't wait to enjoy your clean room later. You have to take immediate action.**

This rings true for running a business, having a good relationship, moving up at your job, and pretty much anything. You have to take the initiative and figure it out. Being a "clean person" is extremely important to success. In my business at the art gallery/ clothing store/event space, cleaning was an essential part of the hourly/daily/ weekly tasks to keep the place from falling apart. I was so frustrated so many times, feeling like I was nothing more than a glorified janitor. That's when I realized that we should glorify the janitor because without a clean space, everything falls apart.

Make your bed in the morning.

Years later, I was laying in bed at my mom's house. I had the garage full of stuff, my room full of stuff, and there I was back at my mom's house at twenty-five and I was lost in the mess. I was, needless to say, depressed about it because I felt at the time that I was too old to be living with my mom. I was still in Texas and I was just miserable. I had finished college and my little sister had signed up to the Peace Corps and was going to Africa. I was full of dreams, but had no plan.

I was laying in bed praying for hours in desperation for an answer. I asked, *"What am I supposed to do, tell me what to do,"* over and over and over again. Finally, out of the blue, I heard a voice, *"Make your bed in the morning."* I jumped out of the bed and immediately broke down in tears. Wherever the voice came from, it was shocking and made an impact in my life that still gives me chills to this day.

Think about it. Make your bed in the morning. What a simple, yet profound thing. While laying there pondering the statement, I thought about what it meant and it really blew my mind. Start right away in the morning, don't procrastinate. Put God first and put yourself first, and don't put it off until later in the day. Who is in the bed with you? Make your bed/home a priority. Get organized. Don't lay around all day and get out of bed in the afternoon. Get up early and get it done. The list of symbolism goes on and on. Make your bed in the morning and do it with intention, and see what an impact it will make on your life.

What happened to me? I made my bed in the morning. Then I cleaned my room. By the end of the month, my sister and I organized a huge garage sale and sold everything that we had. That's the day I made the rule: if it doesn't fit in my car, then I don't need it. My sister was off to Africa and I was moving to Los Angeles. What did I do first? I woke up that next morning and I took immediate action. A great place to start is to make your bed.

Drop in the bucket theory, one step at a time.

All big achievements are a series of smaller achievements. Nothing happens all at once and, even if it is happening at the same time, the tasks are divided by multiple people. Understand that you have to lay one brick at a time to build a wall and the same goes for anything. The key is that you don't have to be the one who does every task. People on your "what do you have" list can help you. Use the intangible qualities that you have to utilize the people around you. These qualities are leadership, vision, initiative, and immediate action.

If you want to do something properly, you have to go through all of the steps. If you break down your large ambition into smaller, bite-size steps, before you know it, you will be making progress. I call it the drop in the bucket theory.

Let's imagine that you have all of your various things that need to happen. If you imagine a faucet dripping, it is steady, consistent, and although each drop is small, before you know it, there is enough water to fill the tub and then overflow and then fill the whole house. Like the second hand ticking while you are waiting for something to happen, you will notice how slowly the time goes by, but when you're not focused on the clock, the time seems to fly by. Your whole life can fly by and you look back and say, where did the time go? The compounding effect of the drop in the bucket theory is how you build an empire.

Let's make this even clearer to drive the point home. The bucket is your clearly defined idea. It is the folder that holds your thoughts, ideas, and progress on a certain long-term project. The drops are small accomplishments or tasks that you might get done on a regular basis. This is a way to keep your focus on a particular activity over a long period of time. These kinds of projects, like working on a book or developing a website or writing a screenplay, which have to be accomplished little by little over time, can seem daunting, but when taken as one small part by one small part, eventually add up to a completed project.

If you think of the drop in the bucket as a negative, like addictions or wasted time, imagine how much loss is slowly stacking up.

To employ the drop in the bucket theory, you have to be steady and consistent and regularly accomplish the smaller tasks that lead to you eventually achieving your major goal. In other words, eventually, you will have a bunch of buckets overflowing with possibility. Then you are far more prepared to seize an opportunity when it manifests itself. Mysteriously, luck finds you.

When you have an idea like going to the gym, for example, you have to take immediate action. You have to do it immediately or you have to schedule it immediately. Then you have to work out one step at a time. When something has to get done, don't say: "Oh, I'll get around to it"; force yourself to get it done immediately. Procrastination is in the definition for bad habits because it is a bad habit that has to be broken, and no one else can break it but you and you alone.

Think of all the hard work that goes into procrastination. By the time you do something, you almost always look back and say *"Shit, what took me so long?"* It takes almost as much energy to sustain a bad habit as it takes to break out of it. Self-drive can be developed through hard work and dedication. It can be developed through building positive habits.

"Start to Swim!"

As I was writing this chapter, a girl told me in a discussion at the gallery that she felt like she was drowning in the ocean every day because she didn't know what to do with her life. I said she was probably dealing with the feeling of powerlessness and living her life from a place of fear. If you're drowning in the ocean, it's probably a good idea to start swimming.

The feeling of wanting to take action is the response to the feeling of powerlessness. Let's admit we are all totally powerless over death, not to mention chance and random shit happening. No one is immune to random things going wrong. The feeling of powerlessness pushes us to try to gain some sense of control over our own destiny. That's why we have to take action as if we are in the middle of the ocean and if we don't swim, we will drown. Are you going to sink or are you going to swim?

We are all in the middle of the ocean, so to speak, when we want to do something about where we are in our life. You look around and feel totally overwhelmed and there is no land in sight. Since there is no land in sight, you may as well just give up, right? What's the use, right? No. You have to dig deep to find that inner spark of hope to keep yourself going. Although I would love to tell you that you are not all alone, the truth is that no one else is going to swim for you; you have to do the work. However, you can reach out to others for help, sometimes when someone is drowning they need someone else's help to get to shore.

Don't Let Opportunity Get Away

I hadn't had a day off in months and had been working over twelve hours every day. I was so exhausted, but somehow when I looked into Katerina's eyes, I knew it was all worth it. How was I going to make it through this? I needed thousands of dollars by the end of the month and was upside down. My stress was through the roof.

As we were breaking down the show, I noticed a couple riding scooters towards the gallery. Then I noticed it was Todd, an old friend of mine from my last apartment in the sky. We had hit it off one morning over coffee and had become friends, but we hadn't seen each other since. I said "Hey, Todd, over here."

He said, "Zach, is that you?" As we got to talking, right in front of my gallery, he told me that he was out looking for art for his new place and was headed over to check out a gallery down the street. I said "No kidding," and turned towards my place. I said, "You don't say, this is my gallery."

He looked at me dumbfounded, "Are you serious? This is unbelievable, can I check it out?" Of course, we went in to check it out.

When we got inside, he was blown away and immediately fell in love with one of my huge and very expensive pieces hanging right in the window. A few days later, he said he wanted to buy it but wanted to see it in his place first. I was floored. It wasn't a deal yet, but it was looking good. He is extremely successful and very well known. He is the type of guy who says what he wants and wants it right now. It was around 7:00 p.m. when he called me. I said, "I'll bring it tonight." But how were we going to get it there? We didn't have a truck and U-Haul was closed.

Be willing to do whatever it takes

I told Van the good news and called Katerina. Todd's place was about a mile away on the other side of Downtown Los Angeles. I showed up at the gallery and I said, "Van and Kwes, we have to do this now." I said, "*We have to carry it.*" Can you imagine Van Vegas and Zach Touchon carrying a massive seven-by-eight-foot piece of art worth thousands of dollars a mile away down the street? It was a sight to see. Van and Kwes switched off and I carried it the whole way. I was determined to make this happen.

We got to Todd's place and it was out of this world. It was on the thirty-third floor and around five thousand square feet. You could see the whole city from the panoramic view. It truly was jaw-dropping and breathtaking. We hung the piece, he loved it, and he bought it.

After selling that piece, we went from upside down and going under to out of the weeds and back on top. We were going to make all of our bills and it was going to be OK. I never felt better than that moment when Katerina looked at me with her eyes filled with a look that can only say, I'm proud of you and I love you.

CHAPTER 11

Know When to Let Go

With my new commitment to stick with what was working, and having the huge help of Van helping out at the gallery, I started to focus on painting. We had the place booked out. I had taken on a new young musician named Jude and was feeling very optimistic about where it was all going. We had done a couple of music videos and, in general, it was going pretty well. I had just landed a big job that was a full renovation of a house on the other side of town and things were really headed somewhere fantastic. It was going great until one morning around 6:00 a.m., when I got a call from Van.

"Zach, you have to get down here, the whole place is flooding."

I jumped out of bed and ran across the street. On the way, I saw a huge part of the street gushing with water and flooding everything around it. Caught in the line of fire was my gallery. I came to find out a 110-year-old pipe busted. The streets were flooded as if it had just rained for several days. I rushed towards the gallery.

The space was a corner retail spot in an old building. It was four thousand square feet with the first level being street level and the second being below ground in the basement. When I got down in the basement, the entire place was flooded. There were Kwes, Van, and Jude trying to stay ahead of the water flowing like a waterfall down all the walls. Jude and Kwes were two young artists I had brought on to develop and they happened to be there, still working on music from the night before.

The next thing I knew, I was all over the news. The headlines read "Local Gallery Destroyed." There I was in the middle of a huge project flipping a four-bedroom house on the interior and exterior on a thirty-day timeline, and now my gallery was destroyed.

After wasting a lot of time trying to get out of my lease and arguing with my landlord, I decided there was no choice but to repair the damage the best I could. I was booked the following week and was running out of time. I decided to get the gallery done while I was juggling the job. I didn't have any other choice.

In retrospect, I may have had the opportunity to walk away at that moment, but I had a ton going on. The landlord assured me that he would come after me if I just left and the whole thing would end up in court. My ex-partner wanted to walk away, but I knew it would be a battle and I just didn't have it in me. The truth is, it just wasn't the right time to walk away. I had to end on a good note.

The whole thing was a complete nightmare that cost me thousands of dollars. Ultimately, we got the gallery done, then the job was done a few days late and the customer wasn't happy. I ended up losing money on the job, as well. Needless to say, I was devastated after having one of the worst months of my entire life.

I was so disappointed in myself. I was back to blaming myself for being an artist. I was right back where I had started. I thought if I wasn't an artist, this wouldn't be happening to me. Katerina was totally amazing. She helped me through the entire process from cleaning the gallery to putting on another art show to raise money and just being there to support me. She helped me stay focused on the positive and push through it.

My accountant had told me that I should focus on the painting company from the very beginning, but I wanted to make the gallery work. One of the hardest things to do is knowing when it is the right time to let go and move on. I had it in my mind that if I just stayed focused on the gallery, it would work and that, at some point, things would start working for me instead of against me. I sat down with Katerina and, after a long conversation, decided that I was going to stop letting the gallery keep me from what was actually making me money, which was painting.

CHAPTER 12

Accept Your Success

If you google failure, you will find...

A simple **definition** of **failure** is: An act or instance of **failing** or proving unsuccessful; lack of success.

Robert Schuller stated these famous words,

"Failure doesn't mean you're a failure; it just means you haven't succeeded yet."

Henry Ford said,

"Failure is only the opportunity to begin again more intelligently."

I am not exactly sure where it came from, but it went something like this:

"Failing is success because you succeeded at failing and that is better than doing nothing at all."

What I say is, if you learn from your failure and become a better person from it, then it was a success. Now you can try again and have a better chance to succeed next time. Inside of every failure are lessons to be learned.

"I've failed over and over and over again and that's why I succeed."-Michael Jordan

In the United States and pretty much everywhere else, for that matter, success is defined by money. The rich guy with a big house, fancy car, and so on, is the successful guy. Success is usually thought to be largely related to material things and getting those things, and only when you are rich are you truly successful. But that's not necessarily true. What I think is **success may be different from what you think success is, and for someone else it may be totally different**.

I'll never forget the time that I learned this lesson the first time. I was twenty-one and in junior college. I was sitting on a bench reading a book when another student walked up to me and asked, "Do you mind if I ask you a question?"

Of course, I said, "Yes. How can I help?"

He said, "I am working on a paper for a class and I am asking a bunch of people a question. May I ask you a question?"

"Yes," I said. "What is it?"

He went on, "What does success mean to you?"

I said, "Well I guess it would mean that you are rich and have a beautiful car and house and..." I stopped for a second and thought about it. Then I went on, "At least that's what most people would say, right?"

He said, "This is your answer."

I said after thinking about it for a moment, "I think success is setting a goal and reaching it. When you set a goal and then go through the steps to get to it, then you are successful. So, I think the truth about success is really about what the goal is. If your goal is to be rich, then you are only successful when you have that. If your goal is something else, then your success may mean something else to you. In that case, I guess success is different for everyone."

He said, "Excellent, thank you." He walked away and that was that.

I sat there and thought about that question a lot and that is when I came up with the concept Accept Your Success. The thing about that moment that really stuck with me was that I was becoming obsessed with the book I was reading and thought it was quite unusual that he would walk up to me at that exact moment. What was the book I was reading? *How To Win Friends and Influence People* by Dale Carnegie. After that, I became obsessed with reading Carnegie, Napoleon Hill, Ziglar, and the like all through my twenties and just fell in love with their philosophies.

So, to get to success, the two most important steps are as follows. Now, remember this is nothing new and I am sure you have heard it in one form or another.

> 1. Set a clear goal and define what you want, be specific, and write it down.

> 2. Make a clear plan on how you are going to get there and write it down.

The best way to never fail is to never have a plan, but that is also the way that you never succeed.

If you google success, this is what you will find: the fact of getting or achieving wealth, respect, or fame; the correct or desired result of an attempt; someone or something that is successful; or a person or thing that succeeds.

"Success is to be measured not so much by the position that one has reached in life as by the obstacles which he has overcome while trying to succeed." - **Booker T. Washington**

In my case, I wanted to own a gallery. I wanted to become an entrepreneur. I wanted to pursue my art career. So, by the time the gallery was coming to an end after three long years, I felt like it was a huge success.

What I mean by accepting your success is to find the positive things inside of what you are perceiving as a failure. Find the things that you did right and recognize them. Understand when you reach your goal that it's never going to be good enough or big enough and you are always going to want more.

"I have not failed. I've just found 10,000 ways that won't work." - Thomas A. Edison

Stop looking at things as failures or successes, and start looking at things from the perspective of what you can get out of it. Because the concepts of failure and success are so subjective, it's important to not get all worked up about it and make it your only focus. A person can drive themselves crazy trying to define if a certain thing was a failure or success. The truth is usually most things are a combination of the two. Look at the things that you have gone through or will go through with the eyes of a student always looking for ways to improve.

"Education is the most powerful weapon which you can use to change the world." **- Nelson Mandela**

Take time to celebrate.

I had met a woman who understood me and was willing to stand by my side through the good times and the bad. One night after hanging out with friends, I dropped to my knee in our bathroom and said, "I can't wait any more, Katerina Khrustaleva, will you marry me?" She embraced me and said, "Yes, I will." It wasn't the mountaintop moment that I had wished for, but it was a memorable moment that we will never forget.

A few months later, we were married and it was beautiful. I felt so much joy and pride when my family was able to be there and see us join together. We were able to afford everything, pay all of our bills, and keep the gallery going at the same time. Van was the one who made all of this possible by being at the gallery when I wasn't.

As a matter of fact, a week before we got married, we booked the gallery on the same day as our wedding. So, I ended up setting up the gallery and the wedding, and Van managed the event while we had our wedding. Then, the next day, I was back to work. It wasn't easy and if I could have had time off, I would have, but I had to do what I had to do to make it all come together.

If I had a chance to do it all over again, I would like to have planned more time to celebrate. I worked the day before the wedding, the day of the wedding, and the day after the wedding. I know that is what had to happen for everything to get paid, but the lesson learned was that in a perfect world, it is important to schedule time to celebrate. When you can squeeze in the time and make it work, do it. Take time to pat yourself on the back and focus on the small victories. With that being said...

Schedule time to not work. Life isn't always about working.

"Do you love life? Then do not squander time, for that's the stuff life is made of." **- Benjamin Franklin**

CHAPTER 13

Learn from Your Mistakes

and Move on

Don't let any particular failure or success be your new running monologue.

When something is over, let it be over. People have a strange tendency to carry the success or failure with them long past the event, whatever it is. This becomes your running monologue and it can have success-killing effects on your next venture. For example, when you are complaining about your last partner, talking about your massive failure, or how bad you were screwed over. Or adversely, when you are bragging about your huge success or the famous person you did business with, what usually happens? The people in your next project or venture are going to hear that, and one of their thoughts will be, "Should I get involved with this person?" I'll tell you a little story to explain exactly what I am talking about.

Katerina and I had just started dating and we were out at an opening of works by Ed Moses at a gallery owned by a good friend of mine named William Turner. Katerina and I were walking around and chatting it up with some of the other people at the show when we ran into a guy who I knew. He didn't exactly remember me, although this would be the fourth time we had met "for the first time." He is an old guy who dresses very flamboyantly with the personality to match. I said hello and introduced Katerina, as any polite person would.

Right away, he began to tell me about who he was. He was the first singer in a major rock band that you have heard of and was replaced by another guy who you have heard of just to become the forgotten guy who nobody has ever heard of. He went on and on about it like it was the first time he had told me. The story is pretty good and cool if you have heard of the band, but Katerina, being born at the height of the band's fame and being from Russia, had no idea what he was talking about. So, after about fifteen minutes, I politely stopped him and said we needed to move on. But it was good to see him.

Honestly, I feel bad for the guy. The third time we met was at a funeral for our mutual friend's father who had passed away. There, he was quiet and actually was very cool and easy to be around. The guy he was there was actually interesting and you could tell that he was a very deep thinker and generally a good guy. You see, at that occasion, he was around old friends and I am sure that they had heard his story a million times and I am also sure they had told him that they were tired of hearing about it.

The lesson is, when you have a failure or a success, let it go and move on. Don't carry it with you and let it become your running mono-logue. What my friend told me was to stop dropping your resume. Stop telling people you just met about all of your failures and your victories. Treat everyone like they are an old friend who is tired of hearing your stories and focus on being a good listener instead.

This is the same in business as it is in personal relationships. Imagine if you talk about your broken heart over and over again to your new girlfriend or boyfriend. What do you think will happen? They won't stick around very long. Keep your new relationships and let your old ones go. I'm not saying you can't talk about things that have happened, but don't make that your running monologue.

When you are done with people, places, things, or intangibles, you need to move on. The old saying comes to mind: ***"It's not how you get knocked down, but how you get back up."*** Guess what? It goes the same for successes as well. You have to constantly renew and find new ways to succeed. If you think that your last success is the greatest success and get the attitude that you have everything figured out, then you will become too comfortable and eventually be stuck in the past. Think about companies who got stuck on their last success and didn't look for new victories. The one that comes to mind is Blockbuster, but there are lots of other companies that got stuck on one model and eventually were put out of business because they were stuck on old successes.

What my brother-in-law told me is that he and his company are constantly renewing and refreshing. What he says to his team is, *"That's it, guys, we are doing everything wrong. Let's wipe the slate clean and start fresh."* This doesn't mean that they are actually doing everything wrong; what it means is to look at it like you are doing everything wrong so you can get a fresh perspective on it. When you think you are doing everything right and there is no reason to change anything, then you end up getting stuck in your ways and stop improving. This doesn't mean changing everything. What it does mean is to look at everything with a new perspective. Fresh thinking can lead to creativity and genius.

This also is a great practice in relationships. People have the tendency to keep doing things the same way over and over again and getting too comfortable in relationships. Katerina and I met a couple one evening that were celebrating sixty years together and they were still in love after all those years. We couldn't help but ask, what is the secret? The answer was very cute and gave us a laugh, but it made a lot of sense. She said "We are still boyfriend and girlfriend." The basic idea is that it is still fresh and new in their minds and they keep that freshness by saying, "Oh, we are still boyfriend and girlfriend." The lesson is to keep it fresh. Try to keep that same spontaneity that you have in a new relationship.

As an artist, I am constantly starting over. Not only with a new piece of work, but with new styles and types of creativity. With music, I am always trying new stuff. This doesn't mean to keep jumping around to new ideas. What this means is keep the spontaneity and creativity flowing by trying to start back at the beginning. Admit that you are not perfect, and that there are still places to improve and ways to explore and experiment.

In every success and failure, there are things you did right and things you did wrong. Take a personal inventory and see what can be improved or removed, but don't ignore it. Take a step down off your high horse after a success or get up and stand up straight after a failure. Look at yourself in the mirror and say,

"Today is an opportunity to start all over again. I am going to approach today with a renewed attitude. I am going to be proud of the things that I have accomplished. I am going to own the things that I have done wrong. I am going to

make a conscious effort to be grateful for what I have and let go of what I had. "

CHAPTER 14

Start Over

IT'S NEVER OVER UNTIL IT'S OVER AND EVEN WHEN IT'S OVER IT'S ONLY JUST BEGUN.

I would love to tell you that there is a magical end to the story where two people run off and live happily ever after, but that's not how this story ends. The truth is, life just isn't that way and it never will be. The truth is, when it's over, it's not really over, it's only just begun. My story may not end like a fairytale, happily ever after. But I am happy, after all. I would go through it all over again if I knew it would lead me back to my wife and the love that we share.

In the end, my wife was the real champion. I hadn't finished the book at that point, but I had started it and, using the principles in the book, she made us thousands of dollars selling anything that was worth something. Some things she sold for five dollars and others she sold for hundreds and hundreds of dollars.

I could have left the gallery a complete disaster and just walked away, but I decided to end on a good note. I did exactly what I did when I was nine years old and started with the trash. By the end, I threw away nearly five tons of things I had been holding on to and it felt amazing. The whole process took a couple of months and a lot of hard work, but we did it together. I left the place after mopping one last time and even let my ex-partner keep the deposit.

After everything was said and done, only a month after the gallery closed, we packed up and moved again. We were done with downtown after everything we had been through. This time, we ended up in Santa Monica near the beach.

The new story was sure to end in riches and fame. There we were with a new event space and gallery twice the size of the previous one and without the burden of rent. We had a beautiful apartment with twenty-five-foot ceilings filled with art and designer furniture. We had a rooftop patio where we could hear the birds sing and watch the clouds float above the city as we watched the beach and felt its breeze. The phone was ringing and the paint jobs were piling up. We were just a week away from everything falling into place when the Covid-19 virus began to spread across the world, causing a global pandemic.

What do you want now?

CHAPTER 15

Fear

"The Greatest Intangible"

When I got to the last part of chapter fourteen, I thought the book was finished. I was so excited I decided to send out the book to a list of people, calling them my mastermind group. The following is the email that I sent:

Hello and welcome to the journey.

I did it! I wrote a book!

This is the first draft of "You Have Everything You Need To Get What You Want." I have been working on it for about six months and now I have completed the first draft. I am very excited to invite you to be a part of my mastermind group.

What is a mastermind group?

Napoleon Hill is clear about the criteria for a Mastermind alliance. He describes it as "Two or more people combining knowledge and effort in a spirit of perfect harmony for the attainment of a definite and specific purpose."

When people with different backgrounds and skill sets come together to help each other achieve their goals, that's a mastermind. Hill addresses the Mastermind in all of his important works including The Law of Success in Sixteen Lessons as well as his classic Think and Grow Rich.

So, I am asking you and a few others to read my new book and give me a review and notes. What is the focus? I am looking for your thoughts not on the exact words per se but just your thoughts on the general idea and the basic principles. Is there something you think needs more thought? Are there ideas that I should add? All ideas are welcome although there is no promise to change anything at all. I really want to make sure that I am doing everything I can to get this book to be the best it can be.

I am hoping that you can read the book as soon as possible so I can move forward with the next steps. I will also be looking for ideas on what to do next but we are not that far yet. Also check out the cover and if you have any ideas on that I would love the input.

After hearing everyone's ideas I will take another stab at it and do revisions. Then I will have the final draft. If you don't want to read it or after reading it, don't want to give notes that is fine as well.

I have asked each of you to be a part of this because all of you are important to my journey for different reasons. You all have different skills and points of view that can really make a big difference. I am honored to be in each of your lives and I hold each of you dear to my heart. Thank you for being in my life and supporting me all of these years.

Thank you,

Zach

Following this email, something truly amazing and unexpected happened. After sending out the manuscript, I was very excited and feeling confident. Suddenly, after sleeping for about an hour, I was awoken by this deep paralyzing fear and anxiety. My jaw was clenching, my heart was racing, I was completely terrified, and I had no idea why. I described how I was feeling to my wife and said, "I feel like I am a scared child, naked and fully exposed for the world to see. Tucked tightly in the corner filled with fear. I feel helpless and I have no idea why."

It was like a shadow was crawling out of me. One that had been there hiding away for years and years. This fear has been holding me back. I can't put my finger on why or what it is or what it means or even how it got there, but it is there. Maybe each of my friends knew that fear was there inside of me and never knew how to put their finger on it either. Maybe we all have that fear. The feeling that we aren't good enough, that we can't do it, that we aren't worth it, that we don't deserve it. Maybe it's a fear of failures or, one that's very hard to make sense of, a fear of success. Maybe it's a fear of the unknown. Maybe it's the child inside each and every one of us that is just desperate to be loved. We want to feel accepted by the world and that we matter, right? I said to Katerina, as tears rolled down like a faucet, free flowing, "Something is happening to me. Something new. Something that makes me uncomfortable and uneasy. I think I'm having a breakthrough."

As I lay there in bed staring at the ceiling, the universe seemed to open up to me and I could see the vastness of space and I was overwhelmed with the feeling that everything is connected. In that moment, I journeyed through time and space and saw through the veil of fear that had been covering the eyes of my soul for potentially most of my life. I'm not sure what happened in that moment, but whatever the feeling was, it was as if the fear, like a shadow, crawled out of me and was released from me, and now I could see far more clearly.

That's when I realized that I was missing maybe the most important chapter of all. The GREATEST INTANGIBLE FEAR. Like Franklin Roosevelt once said, *"**There is nothing to fear but fear itself.**"*

Fear is so elusive and like a monster hiding in a corner, waiting to hold us back from what we want. What I realized is that now that I know it's there, I have this overwhelming need to face it, overcome it, and conquer it.

There are many types of fear. The fear of death, the fear of being judged, the fear of success, the fear of failure, the fear of losing, the fear of losing love, the fear of being incapable, the fear of the unknown, the fear of not being good enough, the fear of how others perceive what you are doing, the fear that no one cares, the fear that you'll never get what you want. All of these types of fear are crippling and keep you from taking action. Fear is like a cage for your soul when it's in its unhealthy form. Fear can be good when it is protecting you, but when it is preventing you from getting what you want, it is unhealthy and destructive.

For me, the fear I was feeling was a combination of many of these. The fear I was feeling had no sound reason and it was not based in reality. It was not clear what it was. It was a feeling that I didn't understand. This fear hides deep inside your subconscious and it is elusive, like a burglar in your home that you have no idea is there.

In this pivotal moment, I realized that I needed to accept that this fear existed and face it. I needed to bring it out, own it, and walk through it. I needed to say out loud *"I'm afraid, but I choose to face it now."*

How could I come up with all of the people, places, things, and intangibles that were holding me back, and I never once mentioned fear? Let's face it, the greatest intangible in all our lives is most definitely fear. Sometimes the fear inside of us can be so crippling, it can lead to a life of total inaction. It can lead to a life of isolation and keep us from loving. It can help us see things not as they are, but as how we perceive them from a perspective of fear. Even though we know that there is fear, we won't face it. We have a fear of fear. It's like if we admit we are afraid, then we are weak. We need to understand that fear is a natural human thing and it's nothing to be ashamed of.

In many cases, this fear is rooted in early life. Although no one remembers learning to walk, we all do it every day without thought. What other things do we not remember learning that are a part of us? I have heard many people say "What's the point of college? I feel like I didn't learn anything." The truth is they did learn and they use that knowledge every day, but they just don't give the credit to education.

I believe that fear is just like this. We may not even remember where we developed the fear that cripples us. When we find ourselves feeling fear that has no base in rationality, we need to rewrite our brains by forcing ourselves into the type of thing that makes us feel this fear. We need to reprogram ourselves by taking action.

When we force ourselves to face our fears, we usually find that it isn't rational, that there is no danger, and we are more courageous than we can imagine.

When I sent out the email, I was on a high and I didn't think about it. I was in the mindset of immediate action. When we give ourselves time to think, what usually happens is that fear starts to build and we say to ourselves, *"I'm not interested in doing this or that or that,"* or *" this isn't for me."* Ultimately, what we like to do is cop out and make excuses when deep down we aren't facing our fear. When we take immediate action, all of the sudden we find ourselves facing the fear. **What we find is that we can overcome our fears, but it takes courage.**

Like I said, fear can be healthy. For example, the fear of being burnt keeps us from being burnt again. Where does this come from? Childhood. And guess what? Most of us don't remember the first time we were burnt. This same type of healthy fear can become unhealthy because our minds like to protect us from things that can cause us danger or discomfort. When we are hurt, we avoid those situations that we think could lead to that happening again and, although this can be healthy, oftentimes it quickly morphs into irrational behavior. For example, someone may have been left by a person that they were deeply in love with and this caused an incredible amount of pain. Now, that same person has developed a fear of being left by someone else. Then this fear keeps that person from ever giving love a chance again. It also leads this person to creating generalizations in their mind and creating negative feelings about themselves and others that have no base in reality.

I believe that this learned fear is the basis for hatred, separation, racism, and so many other things in this world that keeps people from getting what they want and, even worse, keeping others from getting what they want. We learned these biases, which may not have any rational basis, and made them a part of ourselves, yet most of the time we don't even remember where they came from.

Is there something that you are afraid of? Is that the actual thing you are afraid of? How do we uncover these deep-rooted fears? How do we bring them out and look at them?

Courage is not the absence of fear; it is the willingness to face that fear and walk through it.

"A coward dies a thousand deaths, but the brave only die once." **- Ernest Hemingway**

Courage is how we face fear. It can be done all at once in a big immediate act. Or it can be faced through a step-by-step process. Look at the thing that you are afraid of and make a conscious decision to do things that help you overcome that fear. Reprogram your mind by realizing that there is nothing to fear except fear itself.

When I realized that I was seeking the approval of others and looking for congratulations for my accomplishments, it came to light that I was dealing with the fear of not being approved, liked, or that people would judge me.

I discovered that I was trapped in the fear that people would think I was unqualified to write such a book. I was afraid of being judged, people not loving me, and not being able to walk my talk. I was afraid that I wasn't good enough, that this would be just another pipe dream, that no one would care, and that I didn't have what it takes. I was afraid of rejection.

The truth is I was like a beaten dog who was afraid that, once again, I would be beaten down with more disappointment.

Then I had a breakthrough. I remembered what I had written in the first part of the book. I'm doing this for myself. Not anyone else. That's when I realized that the only important thing was to do the best I could and then push past any self-imposed limitations I had put on myself.

So, I began to take action. Much of my fear is fueled in part by social media, seeing others doing better than me or looking better than me or having a better life than me. I was worried that my story wasn't important. So, I began to put out messages. I would record videos and put them out. The requirement was that I wasn't able to think about what others thought; I would just focus on honesty and facing my fear of approval. What happened? People thought it was great. I started to touch people and help them have revelations. What I realized was that there was nothing to fear. I am not in control of what other people think about me. I'm not in control of so many things that I was afraid of. You see, most of my fears were based on "what ifs". What if people don't like me? What if nobody buys the book? What if, what if, what if? It is madness and definitely compares to insanity. What I like to do now is put a positive twist on the what ifs and it helps me gain courage. What if I'm a huge success? What if the book actually helps people? What if all my fears are completely irrational?

What if you face your fears? Are you going to die? Will you be hurt? What if you are a success? Is everyone going to hate you? What if nobody cares? Guess what, none of this matters.

Don't focus on the fear, focus on facing the fear. Don't focus on things that you are not in control of. Focus on what you are in control of.

There I was with it all on the line and the fear was huge. The coronavirus had swept across the world. All our business vanished into thin air. Once again, there I was about to lose everything, and this time I was going through it with the love of my life. I was down to fifty bucks and had no idea how I was going to wiggle my way out of the situation.

I called my family, every one of them. My big sister had to lend me some money for food. Fear was everywhere. I even said, "Dad, I'm so afraid right now. I think we might be going under for real this time."

He said to me, "Zach, you made it this far. After all you have been through, you think this is going to take you down? You're the only person I have ever known that can step into a pile of shit and walk away smelling like roses." We had a laugh and I was inspired. I said, "You know what? We are going to make it no matter what it takes."

Once again, my wife was the champion. We began to sell anything else we hadn't sold. We began marketing the painting company. We began putting out flyers. We just became relentless, taking action. Through the process, we found a collector who bought several pieces for her collection. We decided no matter what, we were going to stay together.

You see, I had this deep fear that if we lost everything, how was my wife going to stick around? I was dealing with the fear of losing love. That can be the most crippling fear. Guess what? It was all in my head. She still loved me and she wasn't going anywhere.

Prime the pump.

We had gotten a call from a woman and she wanted her place painted. But she wanted it for a good deal and when I say that, I mean it was going to be very hard to make any money. When there is nothing going, it is important to understand the theory of priming the pump.

When you first stick a pump into a pond, you have to prime it. That means that you have to get the water going. Many times, the first thing that comes out of the pump is mud and dirty water. But once the pump gets going, before you know it, it is flowing water with little effort. Basically, what this means is that when you're getting something going, the first part is usually the hardest part and, more often than not, it is the part that brings up the mud. But once you are rolling, the pump does all the work for you.

On this job, I allowed her to negotiate way below market price or, in my business of painting, I underbid the job. You see, my wife wasn't the only one counting on me. My workers all needed to make rent too. Using this job that I ultimately took a loss on, I was able to build momentum and we just kept working around the clock marketing. Then that client got us a job down the street as part of her helping us make up for the loss and, while we were doing that job, the phone began to ring. Before you know it, the water was flowing and in the middle of a pandemic.

How did this job happen? My wife was selling our bed frame, which we didn't really have space for. The lady that bought our bed was a very nice woman named Susan. Through Susan's recommendation, we got a number of jobs. This shows that, as you take action in the direction of your goal, in my case painting, luck has a way of finding you.

So, when in fear, take action and be relentless. Be unwilling to give up. Keep showing up and be willing to do the hard work of priming the pump.

In order to face your fear, you need to start with brutal honesty. You have to look deep inside of yourself and uncover the fear that lies deep inside you. When you are in a situation where you find yourself gripped with fear and anxiety, you have to walk through it and face it. Look at yourself through different eyes and you will see that there is nothing to fear. When you have that moment when you overcome your fear, you are finally free of it and, although it still comes up from time to time, it is no longer crippling you.

Creating positive mantras can be a very helpful tool to gather your courage. You have to say it out loud.

"I am afraid but I will walk through my fear. I will face my fear. I have the courage and the strength to overcome my fear and conquer it. I will be a pillar of strength for those around me by being an example of a person who faces their fears. I will not let fear hold me back any more."

Then it is good to follow this up with positive affirmations that help to reprogram your subconscious to recognize your fear and face it. Positive affirmations are the opposite of beating yourself up. It's building yourself up. It's pumping yourself up to face your battle. **Be the warrior who chants for victory as he/she marches into battle. Never back down. Never give up**.

You have the power to change everything, so believe in yourself and gather your strength to get up and go get what you want. Don't let anything hold you back.

Maybe you craved the love of a parent who you feel didn't give you that love. Maybe it's your father or mother who abused or abandoned you as a child. Now, this fear makes you avoid love or treat your children in a similar way. Why should you let that fear keep you from love now? Why should you let that fear keep you from being happy now? Recognize it, pull it out, look at it. Better yet, do something about it.

Maybe you were told that you were not good at something. Now, you won't give it a chance because that fear keeps you from taking action. Don't let what people told you in the past keep you from getting what you want. Who cares if nobody approves? Do it for you. Focus on being great for you; don't focus on being great for others. When you are being great for you and you find success, those same people will say, "Wow! I guess I was wrong." At that point, if they don't, then guess what? Put them on your what's holding you back list.

Fear cannot be ignored. It must be faced. It must be overcome. The only person that can do it is you.

You deserve a good life. You deserve success. You deserve to be loved. You deserve to get what you want.

Have an easy day.

One thing that fear helps you do is to put a crazy amount of pressure on yourself. One day, my wife said to me, "Let's make this an easy day." I kept that focus all day. I even told my guys that we were going to have an easy day. That switched my perspective and, if anything came up, I would just say, let's have an easy day. It works. So, when you get up in the morning, think to yourself, let's have an easy day. This is about setting your intentions. Set your intentions to have a positive attitude, spirit, and work ethic. Set your intentions to deal with stressful situations in a way that doesn't stress you out. Set your intentions to make things easy, not difficult.

Fear is like a veil that we place over our eyes and this veil changes the way we perceive reality. When you're coming from a place of fear, the reality that you perceive is altered by your anticipation of the manifestation of your nightmare. When you fear how others may feel, all of a sudden you find judging eyes everywhere you look. When you are in fear of losing love, all of a sudden you see mischief all around. When you are in fear of being taken advantage of, all of a sudden you see mistrust in everyone's eyes. Guess what? You can even attract the negative outcome by creating it. How does this happen? **Fear.**

What we do is reinforce our fears with these new experiences and now we have programmed our minds to live in fear, and we have all the proof we need to back it up. Fear creates expectations, and when you are looking for evidence, you tend to find evidence you want to find. Now, your mind tells you that you are right to be afraid.

"Those who are successful overcome their fears and take action. Those who aren't (successful) submit to their fears and live with regrets." – **Jay-Z**

Face the fear. Embrace a new reality. Remove the veil. A new reality emerges. A reality with endless possibility where you see opportunity when it arises and have the courage to take advantage of the moment. While you are taking action towards facing your fears, all types of new opportunities can and will emerge that you would never expect or never would have been able to see had you never lifted the veil of fear covering your reality.

Be relentless.

Use your fear for drive. Make your fear your strength. Let your courage be your shield.

You have the power to change everything.

CHAPTER 16

A Few Other Things I

Learned Along the Way

Always have a deadline

Everything needs a deadline. You need a deadline, your team needs a deadline, and anytime there is something that needs to be achieved, it needs to have a deadline.

After sending out my first draft, I thought for sure people would read the book and deliver notes in no time. But as of this writing, nearly four months later, only my closest friend Jessie and my wife had responded. After about a month, I got all upset and was about to write an email. That's when I stopped. What can I learn from this experience?

Remember that in every experience, there are two choices when it comes to getting something out of that experience. You can choose to learn something, not take it personally, and see where you can improve. Or, you can choose to learn nothing, take it personally, and keep doing what you've always done. I decided to learn something.

Rarely deadlines are met, they are usually flexible, and because of this in general nobody takes them seriously. When there is a deadline, you have a goal, a stopping point, a place to say, so where are we? When deadlines are dead serious, it is important to express that seriousness to the team and to yourself. They call it a deadline because you are dead if you don't cross the line in time. That means if you don't make it to the deadline, then you ran out of time and you lost.

Not all deadlines are that serious, but if we take them that seriously, a lot more can get accomplished. I like to make my own "imaginary" deadlines. Ones that I make feel like there are serious consequences if I don't accomplish them in time. I literally get the feeling that if I don't accomplish my goal in time, then I will die. I know that adds a lot of potentially unnecessary pressure and stress, but that's what it takes sometimes; it's a good way to create drive. Deadlines hold no power if they don't have consequences. For example, "if you don't turn your homework in on time, then you fail the class," or "if you don't turn in your work on time, you're fired." Adversely, they also work with rewards and the possibility of losing those rewards, for example, "if you turn your homework in on time, you are guaranteed to pass," or "if you turn your work in on time, you get a bonus."

If you read the email again, you will see I should have said something like "Hello everyone, I finished my book. I'm asking everyone to read and give notes. The deadline is one month from today. If you deliver in time, you will be given a thank you in the book and your notes could end up helping the book. I hope to be able to include your valuable input. Please let me know as soon as possible."

Always have a deadline and, when making deadlines, make sure there are consequences or ultimately no one will take it seriously. If there is no deadline, then no one will take it seriously because there is no motivation. Make deadlines, then meet those deadlines and you will have a better chance to get what you want.

We all have this habit of giving ourselves deadlines that are very reasonable. In other words, we give ourselves plenty of time to accomplish things. Then what we like to do is ask why it is taking so long to get what I want. If you want to get what you want and you want it faster, give yourself unreasonable deadlines and try to reach that goal. What you will find is that you can accomplish things way faster than you realize. Getting what you want takes decisions and, making those decisions quickly, you have to be decisive. The quicker you make decisions, the quicker you accomplish your goals. You can force yourself to make decisions more rapidly when you give yourself unreasonable deadlines. Remember, only you think it's unreasonable. Is it really?

Manage expectations

You can't expect anyone else to have the same expectations as you. If you expect others to have the same expectations as you do, then you are setting yourself up for disappointment. For this reason, it is expressly important to be very clear with others about your expectations. Make it very clear what you expect people to do, say, or achieve, or you will most likely be disappointed. When others don't meet your very clear expectations, then you know you are not on the same page and they may be keeping you from your goal. When other people don't meet our unclear expectations, even though we are unclear and the other people may not even have any idea there are expectations, guess what? We take it personally. When we take it personally, it's important to check ourselves and ask ourselves honestly, "Was I clear about my expectations?"

When the answer is, "No, I didn't make that clear," then ask yourself, "Why are you taking it personally?"

Don't take it so personally and don't try to figure out what other people are thinking.

When we take things personally, what we like to do is try to guess what other people are thinking. Sometimes even when we don't take things personally, we are trying to figure out what other people are thinking. No matter when you do it, the cold hard fact is that you are almost always going to be wrong. You may be worried about what someone else is thinking for years, and guess what? They probably haven't even given you or whatever it is you're thinking about a second thought.

Trying to figure out what other people are thinking is a complete waste of time. Once again, this is something you cannot control, focus on what you can control. Most importantly, don't make a bunch of assumptions about what other people are thinking and then start taking it personally, thinking you have it all figured out. Once again, you are usually wrong. What happens is that you look for evidence of your assumption. Then, when you find what you are looking for, that backs up what you have created in your mind. Now, you are trapped in a potential misconception. Don't try to figure out what other people are thinking.

Most people tend to be procrastinators and not go-get-ters, especially when there is no personal interest.

You might be on a mission. You may be relentless. You may be motivated. You may have an inner drive that has no room for procrastination. But getting other people on the same page is going to be very frustrating. Guess why? It's because the vast majority of people in the world and yes, this includes us as well at times, are generally procrastinators, and just generally not go-getters, especially when there is no personal interest.

I touched on this earlier in the book, but here it is again. In general, most people are super self-interested. We generally only care about what we care about. We generally are motivated to action when we, meaning the individual, has something to lose or gain. We can find the presence of self-interest in even the most selfless acts. There is always something that appeals to this self-interest in the actions and choices we make, in particular the prioritizing of our time and energy, putting our self-interest on the top of the list.

If you have ever faced a big obstacle, a major challenge, a huge opportunity, a big project, or something that requires the cooperation of people, you definitely understand the frustration when those around you are procrastinating. When you are "on that mission" and you are ready to take on the world, it drives you crazy. Then, you take it personally. You see, we are driven by self-interest. At that moment, you are on that mission and you want to get to the goal. You want to make it perfect. You want to get it done on time. What about the people around us? What do they want?

Leaders who understand that people are driven by self-interest recognize it, get out ahead of it, and use it to their advantage. They find ways to make the people on the team feel invested on a personal level so that they have the motivation to get on the same page with the bigger picture and ultimately stop procrastinating. Helping people find the motivation can be done the same way that we discussed earlier in deadlines. Add weight to the idea, project, or task that isn't all about what you want. Think about what other people desire and find a way to help them get it. But, keep in mind, the only way for them to get to their goal is to help you get to where you want to go. When you have the mindset to help others get what they want, you increase your chances of getting what you want. Don't forget, relationships are built on reciprocation.

Don't think that your friends, family, and close associates are your target audience.

We all like to ask for advice. We either trust one person or ask a bunch of people and make a decision based on all the input we can get. Although there is nothing wrong with asking for advice because this absolutely is very valuable and necessary, don't assume that the people you are asking are your "target audience." For example, if your friend doesn't like your song, then nobody will like your song. If your friend thinks that nobody will buy what you're selling, then he's probably right and you should just give up. Wrong!

In the world today, we are so inundated with information and products and songs, and books, and you name it, that it is more likely there is a market for what you are selling than not. I like to tell a story that my Grandmother Carol told me a few times.

She was working at a furniture store and, one day, the delivery guys showed up with a bright orange couch. My grandmother said it was the ugliest couch she had ever seen. She went on and on about how bad it was and she had no idea why they put it on dis- play in such a prominent place. She laughed and joked with her coworkers about the fact that nobody would ever buy such an ugly couch. The next day, she was working when she heard somebody say, "Wow, I absolutely love that couch." As she turned around, she was shocked with amazement; it was the overpriced ugly orange couch. She was blown away that they bought the whole set. She said, "Zach, there's a market for everything. Just because I don't like something doesn't mean somebody else won't love it." That was a great insight for me, which really freed up my mind to take some risk and just focus on being great. The market will find you even if you are an ugly orange couch.

Just because the people around you seem to be uninterested in what you are doing, don't take it personally. They are probably just not your target audience. If you believe in what you are doing, go for it and you will find your audience. When you believe, you achieve.

You wanna be great? Start with being grateful.

Wake up in the morning and say out loud as you stretch, "Wow, what a life." Take a deep breath and start your day with an attitude of gratitude. If you start with being grateful for what you have, you may realize you already have everything you want. You just don't recognize it. I said this earlier, but I'll say it again: why is the world going to bless you with more stuff if you don't even appreciate the stuff you already have?

Don't be a slave to debt. Debt is trash, clean it up first.

I talked about this a lot earlier when I said that "when you want to get something going, you need to start with the trash." Debt is your financial trash and it has to be cleaned up first. It's one of the hardest things to do because, as your cash flow increases, so do your wants. As you get more, you want more. But if you are carrying debt, in particular high-interest debt like credit cards, then you need to gain the discipline to overcome that debt first. This doesn't mean all debt is bad. This doesn't mean don't use financing as a way to make certain things happen. What this does mean, just to be clear,

High Interest Debt = Trash.

When the money comes in, just pay the debt. Although it is difficult, we have to get rid of it first. Credit cards can be great if they are used properly, but if not, then they are slowly enslaving you to the financial institutions that you borrow from. In the early days of the United States, we had indentured slavery. I googled indentured slavery and this is the definition:

> *An indentured servant or indentured laborer is an employee (indenturee) within a system of unfree labor who is bound by a signed or forced contract (indenture) to work without pay for the owner of the indenture for a period of time. The contract often lets the employer sell the labor of an indenturee to a third party.*

Maybe I'm crazy, but this sounds a lot like owing money to the bank. We sign a contract, spend the money, then in essence work for the bank. Guess what? They can even sell that debt to someone else. You work and earn the money to make the payment on the interest and potentially continue working for the bank forever. That's how it's set up. So, break the chains of financial slavery and free yourself from the debt. Debt is trash and when we are talking about a "clean house and a clean mind" in reference to our financial house, high interest debt is trash and it needs to be cleaned up first.

Covid-19 hit us hard. Like I said, we were all the way broke. I called my credit card company and, after a long wait, I finally talked to someone. My cards were maxed out and I was really up against the wall. I pleaded for an extension and I'll never forget how I felt when they said yes. I literally began to cry. I look back on that moment and I think to myself, I don't ever want to feel like that again. Credit is really good when you need it, and you find that out really quickly when your back is against the wall.

It's ok to say no. No deal is better than a bad deal.

When you are getting the ball rolling, it's important to have an attitude of "I'm here, I'm yes, I'm ready for success," but it is also important to understand when you need to say "No."

When things were at their worst during the beginning of the corona-virus pandemic and I had to "prime the pump," I was in a position where I had to be willing to do the hard work and potentially take a loss. But I had to come to the point where I had to say "No."

Like Miles Davis once said, *"It's not the notes you play* [that make a song great], *it's the notes you don't play* [that makes it great]." That's the thing, it's not always about the jobs you do take that make you successful. More often, it is the jobs that you don't take that make you successful. Why is this? It is because your time and energy are limited. When you waste time and energy on something that you should have said "no" to, then you are simply wasting time and energy. That is why no deal is better than a bad deal.

Are you charging enough?

I was standing in the backyard of the woman's home that I talked about earlier where I had taken a job that was going to be tough to make money on, and she took me to the side and asked me, "Zach, are you charging enough?" I didn't realize it at the time, but this moment was a pivotal moment that would change my reality and begin a new path that would eventually lead to my financial freedom. Looking back, I think, *"Wow, what a blessing."* I followed my heart to do the job because I just really liked the couple and I knew I was in the right place. But I didn't know why.

She told me I needed to double my prices. My bid was one of the lowest bids she got out of ten different contractors. She is a very powerful woman, spiritually, and I agreed that I needed to raise my prices. So, I gained the courage and doubled my prices. My business exploded.

I wasn't charging enough. Can you imagine realizing how much money you must have left on the table over the years? Instantly, my perspective changed and I realized that for people to take you seriously, you need to charge the right prices. Make sure you are charging enough for whatever it is that you are doing, and remember that your time and energy are limited. Don't get hung up on what you didn't do in the past; focus on what you're going to do about it in the future.

Nobody is perfect

We all want to be great. We all want to do things the right way. But some of us have to have things perfect. Perfection is something that can really hold you up. You see, nothing is ever perfect for the most part, and if you wait until everything is perfect for you to take action, then you are keeping yourself from getting what you want. You have to be willing to suck. That takes bravery. That takes courage. You are not striving for perfection; you are holding yourself to impossible standards. You will never be perfect.

Guess what? We all make mistakes and the road to greatness is an ever-refreshing cycle. This is what makes us human. Beauty is found in imperfection. Realize you don't need to be perfect. The song doesn't need to be perfect. The art doesn't have to be perfect. The script, the movie, the video, the clothes, the...you get the picture. **Don't try to be perfect, strive to be great.** Take action and continuously improve.

CHAPTER 17

Final Thoughts

There is no magical fairy dust that you can sprinkle and make it all OK. There's no quick fix. There's no easy way out. It is going to take hard work.

It is time to make a decision. Do you want to be great? Do you want to have a beautiful life that is fulfilling and rewarding? Do you want to have love in your life and have happy, healthy relationships?

It's time to take responsibility.

You have to be the one who makes it happen. You have to be willing to take responsibility for who you are, where you are, and who you're with. You have to shift your perspective and start fresh by rewiring your brain. Reading this book is a great start, but now it is time to take action.

Just Start!

Stop making excuses about why you are unable to begin your journey to greatness. Just start. Take action. You'll figure it out. But if you keep making excuses about why you can't start, then you are just wasting time. Why are you wasting so much time? Dive in and be willing to make mistakes. Be willing to suck and, eventually, if you don't give up, you will suck less and less.

Don't let fear hold you back anymore. Recognize it and gain the courage to overcome it, and even make it one of your strengths. Be brutally honest with yourself and stop being afraid of fear.

Don't let bad habits rule your life anymore. Take action to remove the negative shit from your life. Why? Because you are worth it and you deserve a healthy, happy, successful, and long life. It's never too late to start fresh. Here is a perfect example.

I was painting a nine-thousand-square-foot mural that I discussed earlier in the book. It must have been around 4:30 in the morning. As I stood on a twenty-foot ladder painting, I heard a shopping cart slowly approaching through the parking lot behind me. As I turned to see who it was that was approaching me, I noticed a man. He was pushing the cart, filled with his belongings, and he said, "Hey man, that's pretty cool. I could never do anything like that."

I turned towards him and I said, "What's your name?"

He responded, "Bill." He went on to tell his story. Bill is a forty-three-year-old white guy who is homeless, hopeless, and hooked on heroin. He's been on the streets for a couple of years, ever since his girlfriend died and then his dog died and he lost his job and then he tried to commit suicide. After getting hooked on pain meds, he slowly turned to shooting up heroin to ease the pain. He sleeps on the sidewalk in a well-lit area to keep from being robbed by one of his neighbors. Everything he owns on planet Earth is inside the shopping cart he pushes around, scavenging Downtown Los Angeles for cans and bottles to get his next fix and maybe even some food if he can afford it.

He watched me for a while as I listened. He had a really bad habit of beating himself up. Telling himself he is worthless. Telling himself that there is no hope. Saying out loud, «God hates me. I'll probably die on these streets."

I finally came down off the ladder and walked towards him slowly. I said, "Listen, Bill, you probably won't make it to be honest. The truth is you are right, you are probably going to die on these streets. I mean look at you, you're pushing a fucking shopping cart around all day. I mean, I would say this is about as bad as bad gets." He looked at me dumbfounded, confused, perplexed even.

Then I continued, "You want to know why? It's because you believe everything I just said, right?"

He nodded, *"Yea, I do."*

That's where I stopped him in his tracks. I said, "That is the root of the problem. Unless you are willing to take responsibility for your life, you're never going to have a chance. You have to stop with all this negative bullshit that you keep telling yourself." He said, "Like what?" I said, "I could never do that, I'm not good enough, I'll never make it. All of these things you tell yourself trap you in your current situation. As you repeat this negative shit to yourself, all day long, you begin to believe it. Why don't we flip that on its head?"

He said, "What?"

I said, "Lie to yourself. Tell yourself you're happy if you're sad and make yourself smile. When your mind says you're not good enough, lie to yourself and say yes I am. Tell yourself all day that you can make it out of your situation and you will find the way. Lie to yourself until you believe it. If you don't do that, then you will forever imprison yourself in your current state. You can make it out. You will if you believe you can."

I packed it up for the night and we said our goodbyes. The truth is, I thought he wasn't listening. I thought that he had no chance.

Fast forward to about two months later. I had a party to celebrate the mural. I was disappointed because only a few people showed up and I just felt terrible about it. Once again, nobody cares about art, right? As the night was coming to an end, I looked towards the front door of the gallery and there was Bill with a note in his hand. I opened the door and there he was, clean shaven and he didn't smell bad. He said to me, "You probably don't remember me—"

I interrupted, "Bill, is that you?"

He said, "It worked, it fucking worked, man. You were right. I know it's not that long, but I have over three weeks off heroin and I found a place to live and I got a job."

I was floored. I said, "Holy shit, man, this is great. I'm so happy for you."

He said, "I don't think you get it, man. You remember that night that I met you and you were painting?"

I said, "Yea."

He said, "I was going there to kill myself. I actually tried to kill myself in that same exact place you were working for the first time when my girlfriend died, that's how I ended up on the street. Anyways, I was going to finish the job that night when we met. But you were there painting and you said what you said. I did it, I lied to myself until I believed it. I just wanted to stop by and say thank you."

At that moment, I realized that although a lot of people didn't show up, it didn't matter. Bill was alive and my mural had done something far more important. Impacting that one person made all of the hours of work worth it for me. The old saying comes to mind, **"If you save one life, you save the world."** In this way, Bill also saved me as well. I looked down at the note and it read, simply, *"It worked. Thank you. Bill."* I began to cry because I was so touched. As the tears rolled down, I knew what I had to do. I had to give it everything I had. What I am doing does matter. It definitely mattered to Bill.

If Bill can make it off the streets and off heroin, then you can make it through whatever you are going through as well. Odds are, if you are reading this book, then you are probably not pushing a grocery cart around the city at the moment. Just take a moment and realize that no matter what situation you are in, you can make it better, but you have to believe you can. You are all out of excuses. It's time for you to get what you want. Don't wait, start now.

You Have The Power To Change Everything!